Nelson Literacy

Series Authors
Karen Hume
Brad Ledgerwood

Series Consultants
Jennette MacKenzie, *Senior Consultant*
Damian Cooper, *Assessment*
James Coulter, *Assessment and Instruction*
Gayle Gregory, *Differentiated Instruction*
Ruth McQuirter Scott, *Word Study*

Series Writing Team
James Coulter, *Assessment*
Judith Hunter, *Instruction*
Maureen Innes, *ELL/ESL*
Liz Powell, *Instruction*
Sue Quennell, *Word Study*
Janet Lee Stinson, *Instruction*
Michael Stubitsch, *Instruction*
Giselle Whyte, *Related Resources*

D1716132

Subject and Specialist Reviewers
Mary Baratto, *the Arts*
Rachel Cooke, *Metacognition*
Phil Davison, *Media Literacy*
Graham Draper, *Geography*
Ian Esquivel, *Media Literacy*
Martin Gabber, *Science and Technology*
Cathy Hall, *Mathematics*
Jan Haskings-Winner, *History*
Maureen Innes, *ELL/ESL*
Dan Koenig, *Health*
Janet Lee Stinson, *Media Literacy*

NELSON EDUCATION

NELSON EDUCATION

Nelson Literacy 8c

Director of Publishing
Kevin Martindale

**General Manager,
Literacy and Reference**
Michelle Kelly

Director of Publishing, Literacy
Joe Banel

Publisher
Rivka Cranley

Managing Editor, Development
Lara Caplan

Senior Product Manager
Mark Cressman

Senior Program Manager
Diane Robitaille

Developmental Editors
Corry Codner
Vivien Young

Assistant Editor
Adam Rennie

Bias Reviewer
Nancy Christoffer

Editorial Assistant
Meghan Newton

**Executive Director, Content and
Media Production**
Renate McCloy

**Director, Content
and Media Production**
Carol Martin

Production Editor
Janice Okada

Copy Editor
Linda Jenkins

Proofreader
Linda Szostak

Production Manager
Helen Jager Locsin

Production Coordinator
Vicki Black

**Director, Asset Management
Services**
Vicki Gould

Design Director
Ken Phipps

Managing Designer
Sasha Moroz

Series Design
Sasha Moroz

Series Wordmark
Sasha Moroz

Series Cover Design
Sasha Moroz
Glenn Toddun

Cover Design
Courtney Hellam
Sasha Moroz

Interior Design
Carianne Bauldry
Jarrel Breckon
Nicole Dimson
Courtney Hellam
InContext Publishing Partners
Jennifer Laing
Sasha Moroz
Jan John Rivera
Bill Smith Design

Art Buyer
Suzanne Peden

Art Coordinator
Renée Forde

Compositors
Carianne Bauldry
Courtney Hellam

Photo Research and Permissions
Nicola Winstanley

Printer
Transcontinental Printing

Series Advisers and Reviewers

Gwen Babcock, Limestone DSB, ON
Jennifer Bach, Burnaby SD, BC
Karen Beamish, Peterborough, Victoria, Northumberland, and Clarington CDSB, ON
Mary Cairo, Toronto CDSB, ON
Maria Carty, Annapolis Valley Regional SB, NS
Joanna Cascioli, Hamilton-Wentworth DSB, ON
Janet Charlton, District 10, NB
Vivian Collyer, Sooke SD, BC
Anne Converset, Niagara DSB, ON
Rachel Cooke, Toronto DSB, ON
Phil Davison, Halton DSB, ON
Connie Dersch-Gunderson, Livingston Range SD, AB
Lori Driussi, Burnaby SD, BC
Judy Dunn, Kamloops/Thompson SD, BC
Eileen Eby, Greater Victoria SD, BC
Ian Esquivel, Toronto DSB, ON
Anna Filice-Gagliardi, Toronto CDSB, ON
Patty Friedrich, London DCSB, ON
Charmaine Graves, Thames Valley DSB, ON
Colleen Hayward, Toronto CDSB, ON
Irene Heffel, Edmonton SD, AB
Phyllis Hildebrandt, Lakeshore SD, MB
Brenda Lightburn, Mission SD, BC
Andrew Locker, York Region DSB, ON
Susan MacDonald, Delta SD, BC
Anne Marie McDonald, Limestone DSB, ON
Beverley May, District 2, NL
Selina Millar, Surrey SD, BC
Wanda Mills-Boone, Ottawa-Carleton DSB, ON
Lorellie Munson, York Region DSB, ON
Barb Muron, Toronto CDSB, ON
Linda O'Reilly, Educational Consultant, BC
Cathy Pollock, Toronto DSB, ON
Gina Rae, Richmond SD, BC
Sherry Skinner, Eastern SD, NL
Susan Stevens, Peel DSB, ON
Janet Lee Stinson, Simcoe County DSB, ON
Melisa Strimas, Bruce-Grey CDSB, ON
Elizabeth Stymiest, District 15, NB
Sue Taylor-Foley, South Shore Regional SB, NS
Laurie Townshend, Toronto DSB, ON
Tracy Toyama, Toronto DSB, ON
Deborah Tranton-Waghorn, Ottawa-Carleton DSB, ON
Ann Varty, Trillium Lakelands DSB, ON
Ruth Wiebe, Chilliwack SD, BC
Mark Wilderman, Saskatoon Public SD, SK
Nadia Young, Toronto CDSB, ON

CONTENTS

Unit 5 — Reality Check

6

12

18

40

47

52

68

74

88

CONTENTS

Unit 6 — Chasing a Dream

Welcome to Nelson Literacy

Nelson Literacy presents a rich variety of literature, informational articles, and media texts from Canada and around the world. Many of the selections offer tips to help you develop strategies in reading, oral communication, writing, and media literacy.

Here are the different kinds of pages you will see in this book:

Focus pages

These pages outline a specific strategy and describe how to use it. Included are "Transfer Your Learning" tips that show how you can apply that strategy to other strands and subjects.

Understanding Strategies

These selections have instructions in the margins that help you to understand and use reading, writing, listening, speaking, and media literacy strategies.

Applying Strategies

These selections give you the chance to apply the strategies you have learned. You will see a variety of formats and topics.

Transfer Your Learning

At the end of the unit, you'll have a chance to see how the strategies you have learned can help you in other subject areas such as Science and Technology, Geography, History, Health, Mathematics, and the Arts.

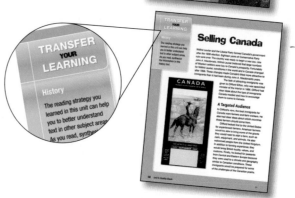

REALITY CHECK

WHAT'S THE DIFFERENCE BETWEEN REALITY AND HYPE?

Unit Learning Goals

- synthesize while reading
- improve fluency in writing

- synthesize while listening
- analyze elements of media texts

- analyze cause-and-effect text pattern

Transfer Your Learning: History

How to → Synthesize

When you synthesize, you combine what you are reading with what you already know. By continually synthesizing as you read, your understanding increases and you gain new perspectives or achieve insights. Sometimes it helps to stop and think about a section or to reread sections.

☑ **Access your prior knowledge of the topic.** For example, if you read the title "Advertising in Disguise," think about what you already know about advertising. As you read, reflect on how the new text adds to your knowledge.

☑ **Make connections between ideas *within* the text.** For example, the introduction to an editorial may express an opinion supported with examples later in the text. Deliberately connect what you thought at the beginning to later ideas. Ask yourself: How does my understanding change as I learn more? Have my opinions changed?

☑ **Compare and contrast ideas in this text with *other* texts.** Ask yourself: Does this text confirm, contradict, or challenge what I know from other reading?

☑ **Consider how the different parts of the text fit together.** Look for relationships in the text. For example, in a story, thinking about how characters, setting, and story events are connected can increase your understanding.

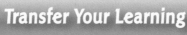

Transfer Your Learning

Across the Strands

Oral Communication: When you are talking with a group, you often hear a number of perspectives on an issue. Which of the above strategies would help you as you listen to differing opinions?

Across the Curriculum

History: In studying history, you may read several accounts of the same event from different perspectives. How does combining several perspectives allow you to synthesize a new understanding of an event?

Talk About It
What does it mean to be cool?

HOW TO ... BE COOL

Satirical Article by Guy Browning

In between being a child and being a parent, the most important thing to be is cool. However, it's incredibly difficult to be cool, because there are no instructions to follow. You can't even decide whether you are cool—other people do that for you.

1. *Stop enjoying yourself*

Simple things you can do. The first and most obvious is to stop enjoying yourself. No one with happy, infectious laughter is cool, because the first priority of cool is to take yourself extremely seriously. Laughing is for people who don't get it. So start scowling and looking at the world with the attitude, "Funny, I think not." If you don't take yourself seriously, no one else will.

2. *Ditch that jaunty walk*

Second, ditch that jaunty walk. Cool people's feet never leave the ground as they are far too weighed down with the awesome responsibility of coolness. Get that spring surgically removed from your step and start shuffling. It goes without saying that cool people don't swing their arms. In fact, any sort of arm movement is a no-no as this could give the impression you are a Scoutmaster.

WHATEVER

NO SCOUTMASTER

3. *Nothing is a good idea*

Synthesizing →

Make connections between ideas within the text. How does your understanding of this satirical article change as you read on? How does your understanding of the author's perspective on cool change?

Never give the impression that you think anything might be a jolly good idea. For example, going out to the cinema might be a jolly good idea, but if you're cool the last thing you would do is suggest it. Decisions like that are made through the sacrifice of the uncool. Only after the uncool have spoken and embarrassed themselves can the cool slump off to the cinema, even though this was the first thing suggested hours ago by an enthusiastic but uncool person who is now at home crying on their own.

NOT COOL

FRESH AIR + SUNLIGHT = UNCOOL

ME!

4. Wear cool clothes

What you wear is critical to coolness. Sturdy easy-care classics don't cut the mustard in the cool department. Cool clothing is always on the thin dividing line between what was absurd yesterday and what will be ridiculous tomorrow. This line is slightly easier to tread once you have established that you are cool. You can then wear a bucket on your head and you will still be cool in the eyes of your less cool friends, who will all come out the next day with buckets on their heads. (This is how the fashion industry works.)

5. Exercise self-absorption

Fresh air and sunlight aren't good for cool as they make you happy and you have to remove your cool clothing. That's why cool people tend to sleep late and come out at night. However, just because it's dark doesn't mean you can't wear your sunglasses. Remember, all eye contact is deeply uncool as it implies a lapse in total self-absorption.

Guy Browning writes the popular "How to ..." column for Britain's weekend *Guardian* magazine. You can find more of his columns in the collection *Never Hit a Jellyfish with a Spade: How to Survive Life's Smaller Challenges.*

← Synthesizing

Compare and contrast ideas in this text with other texts. Does this section confirm, contradict, or challenge what you know about being cool?

← Synthesizing

Consider how the different parts of the text fit together. How do the steps build on one another? How do the images support the text?

Synthesizing

Use a graphic organizer like this one to help you as you synthesize.

Ideas or Information in the Text	What I Already Know	What I Think Now

Reflecting

Synthesizing: After reading this text, what new understanding do you have about being cool? What changed? What caused the change in your understanding?

Metacognition: What helped you synthesize this selection? How did synthesizing help you respond to this selection?

Critical Literacy: Illustrations usually reflect the writer's tone. What tone is communicated with the illustrations in this selection? How would you change the illustrations to create a different tone?

Talk About It
What do you think the title means?

ADVERTISING IN DISGUISE

Nonfiction Article by Shari Graydon

Has anybody ever tried to trick you into eating good-for-you food that you didn't like by disguising it as something else? By slipping spinach in between the layers of your lasagna, perhaps, or putting dates in your favourite cookies?

Advertisers are also wise to this strategy. They know that the more conscious you are of the fact that they're trying to sell you something you may not need, the harder it will be to convince you to buy. So they're always on the lookout for new and unusual places to sneak in a promotional message, without making it obvious that that's what they're doing. They dress up their sales pitches in all sorts of "costumes" by giving them bit parts in popular movies, making them look like programs or news stories—or even paying the person next to you to rave about their products.

Modern advertising disguises are a lot more subtle than this cheesy chicken mascot handing out restaurant menus.

GUERRILLA MARKETING

Some of these strategies are referred to as "guerrilla" (pronounced *gorilla*, but having to do with rebel fighters, not apes!) or "stealth" marketing campaigns. These terms underline the sneakiness of the approach.

Is it fair to try to sell a new cellphone by having a bunch of "cool" actors playing with the phone in public places?

For example, Sony Ericsson Mobile Communications once hired 60 actors and provided them with their newest camera cellphones. Then Sony got them to hang out at popular tourist attractions like the Empire State Building in New York and Seattle's Space Needle. But the actors weren't being paid to see the sights. Cast as fake tourists, their job was to ask unsuspecting passersby to take their pictures. Another 60 actors were hired to hang out in trendy bars, engage strangers in conversation, or play with their phones in a part of the bar where they would attract attention. The point was to get people talking about the new cellphone without letting them know that the "owners" of the product were simply being paid to promote it.

This approach received mixed reviews. Some consumer activists thought the practice was dishonest and shouldn't be allowed. They argued that the actors should have had to wear Sony Ericsson T-shirts or told people they worked for the company. But the marketing firm that dreamed up the idea defended it, saying the actors weren't trying to sell the product, just demonstrate it.

What do you think? Would it bother you if you found out only by accident that the person you were talking to about a new bike or computer game was being paid to tell you it was great?

The Harajuku neighbourhood of Tokyo, Japan, is a cool-hunting hot spot. The kids may look extreme, but elements from their outfits have spawned countless trends.

THE "COOL HUNT"

Another guerrilla marketing approach involves advertisers taking advantage of the influence kids have over each other. They start by seeking out teenage fashion leaders to find out what's considered rad, or hot, or cool. Advertisers call this the "cool hunt."

It works like this: Companies such as Reebok go looking for cool kids in big cities like Toronto, New York, and Hong Kong. They go into the hippest stores or clubs seeking out kids who are so cool that they don't follow fashion trends, they create them.

The companies find out what these kids are interested in—whether it's bleached hair, vintage clothing, or a new kind of music. They ask the kids what they think about a new product they're starting to make and get feedback about how it could be made to look more cool. And then they go back to their factories and quickly begin manufacturing and advertising based on the advice they've gotten from cool kids.

The companies are counting on other kids, who look up to and follow the lead of the cool kids, to buy those products.

Adults who hang out with young people are also recruited to be walking/talking ads. One company gave its new brand of athletic shoe to a carefully selected group of school basketball coaches in the United States. In exchange for the free shoes, the coaches had to promise that they would promote the shoes to all the kids they coached.

Movies are another popular hiding place for sneaky advertisers. Have you ever seen *E.T.: The Extra-Terrestrial*? It's become one of the most popular movies of all time. It also represents a landmark case in the history of advertising.

The producers of *E.T.* approached the makers of M&M's chocolate candies and offered them an opportunity to have their candy featured in the movie. M&M's turned down the invitation. Instead, when the film opened on thousands of movie screens across North America and eventually around the world, a supporting role was given to Reese's Pieces candy. In a now-famous scene, the young boy in the movie leaves a trail of Reese's Pieces candies in his backyard in order to entice the alien E.T. into his house.

As a result of the movie appearance and the "tie-in" advertising that promoted both the candy and the film, sales of Reese's Pieces candy soared by more than 60 percent.

Did you think they just really liked Coca-Cola? Coca-Cola pays millions to have their product featured prominently in every *American Idol* show.

Movies haven't been the same since. Product placements have become more and more common. They can be as simple as a Diet Pepsi bottle sitting on someone's desk in a scene, or a character referring to a particular store. Budget Rent-a-Truck had a starring role in the popular *Home Alone,* and the James Bond film *Die Another Day* took the trend to an extreme, giving screen time to Visa credit cards, Omega watches, Sony Ericsson electronics, Ford cars, and Norelco razors. In fact, some critics and moviegoers objected to having to pay to watch what they said looked more like a two-hour commercial than a movie!

TV shows also accept ad dollars in exchange for putting products in front of the camera. Sitcoms and reality-based TV series have featured everything from cereal and cars to hairspray and electronic equipment. Scriptwriters for the long-running ABC soap opera *All My Children* came up with the idea to incorporate the cosmetics company Revlon into three months' worth of the show's episodes. Even though Revlon employees were referred to by one of the program's characters as "vultures," the company paid several million dollars for the increased profile it got through the show.

Ads are all over sporting events, too. Do these Russian hockey players represent a sponsorship wave that will soon be seen in Canada? Where does the trend of wearing ads stop?

Bogus Mind Control at the Movies

In the 1950s, people got very excited about a thing called *subliminal advertising*. James Vickery of New Jersey said he'd fixed up a movie projector with a special device that flashed the words "Eat popcorn" or "Drink Coke" onto the screen in the middle of the movie. The words supposedly appeared so quickly and for such a brief time that viewers didn't notice them. This is where the term *subliminal* comes in; it means "something that you're unaware of." Vickery claimed that as a result of this new form of advertising, soft-drink sales increased by 18 percent at the theatre and popcorn purchases shot up by 57 percent!

You can imagine the reaction: Advertisers couldn't wait to try it out, ordinary people became afraid that they were going to be brainwashed, and some governments immediately forbade theatres and TV stations from using the technique.

As it turned out, the whole thing was a big hoax. When some researchers attempted to test the device and measure the effectiveness of subliminal advertising, they found that it didn't even work!

DON'T TRY THIS AT HOME!

Next time you're watching a movie or TV show, keep an eye out for product placements, and count up how many you see. Compare the exposure a product gets in a TV show to the kind of profile it might be given in a commercial. Which one are you more likely to remember or talk about with friends? Do you have to hear a sales pitch in order to be persuaded? And does it make a difference to the audience whether it's a villain, a hero—or an alien!—using the product?

Reflecting

Synthesizing: This selection concentrates on stealth marketing campaigns and advertising. What information in the text helped you see advertising in a new way?

Metacognition: What strategies from page 2 did you find most helpful as you synthesized while reading this selection?

Media Literacy: In your opinion, which of the advertising techniques described here has the greatest potential for selling a product?

Behind the Hype

Online Article from CBC's *Street Cents*

What you see is not always what you get. *Street Cents* investigates the truth of fashion and celebrity photography and finds that digital manipulation is a part of nearly every photograph you see.

What Does Retouching Include?

Street Cents has found that almost all fashion and celebrity photos are retouched, so you can take comfort in the fact that the "perfect look" of celebrities is not how they look in real life. Through computer technology, digital artists are able to alter photos like never before. While all digital artists were quick to point out to *Street Cents* that photographs have always been altered, it's easier, cheaper, and more acceptable than ever to make people look as "perfect" as possible.

So, what are digital artists doing to photos? *Street Cents* spoke with retouchers who are responsible for making celebrities beautiful and they filled us in on the most common retouching practices to the most extreme.

> "I really don't see anything sinister in this. It's been going on for years. Essentially, we all want glamour."
>
> — *Dylan Jones, editor-in-chief, British* GQ

Kate Szatmari, a Toronto-based retoucher for celebs such as Kanye West, P. Diddy, Hilary Duff, and Avril Lavigne, told *Street Cents* that she makes changes to every photo that she is given.

Szatmari adjusts the colours and contrast; removes any dirt, dust, and distractions; removes all blemishes; evens out skin tone, removes any wrinkles; and tones down and smoothes any bumps on the celebrity's skin. She also whitens the teeth and eyes, de-wrinkles the clothes and trims off any fat from the body. And she's not done yet!

Models and celebrities are also lengthened and thinned out, although sometimes weight has to be added to very thin models, and heads and bodies are sometimes switched around on a celebrity in order to get the perfect photo, but only cuts from within the same shoot. All digital artists that we spoke to were adamant that they would never put a celebrity's head on a different body and try to pass it off as the celeb's own. Some retouchers will however do this, making such extreme changes to celebrities who want to appear perfect, that the celeb in the photo no longer resembles themselves.

The Celebrity Make Over

Some celebrities have spoken out against the retouching of their photos and extreme celebrity retouching.

Tyra Banks stated in an interview with *CNN Morning News* on April 3, 1998, that she has cellulite and stretch marks and that she "disappoint[s] people who meet [her] in person because [she doesn't look like herself]." What Tyra means is that she doesn't look like her retouched photos. Did you really think she did?

A subtle retouch creates an impossible standard.

Jennifer Aniston told *Vanity Fair* in her May 2001 interview that "the media creates this wonderful illusion—but the amount of airbrushing that goes into those beauty magazines, the hours of hair and makeup! It's impossible to live up to, because it's not real." It's about time people started admitting it!

Nelly Furtado, in October 2002, went public with her disgust over her photo treatment in *FHM* magazine. The full-length black T-shirt she was wearing in the original photo was digitally cut in half to give the effect of a crop top and a fake belly was inserted to attract the magazine's male audience. However, Nelly had not given *FHM* a photo shoot, nor permission to use her picture in their magazine, never mind on the cover. Nelly released a statement in her official fans forum news page in response, writing, "I'm really not happy with *FHM*. In the magazine they say they had a photo shoot with me but I didn't do a shoot with them. They've also airbrushed my body and changed my body shape and I didn't give permission for anything like that."

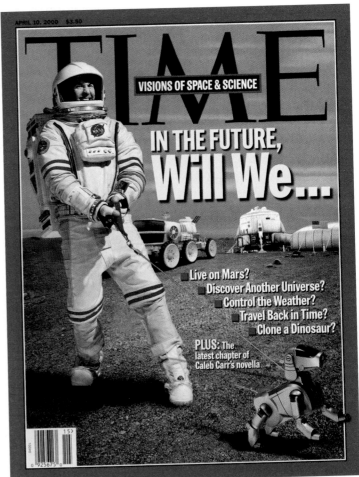

Even responsible and serious news magazines will fake photos to make a point.

Is this a genetically altered camel? No, it's just a digitally altered photo.

Crediting Retouched Photos

Things would be a lot easier on our egos if magazines credited, right on the photo, whether it was retouched or not. However, this is rarely done and probably won't become popular any time soon. Readers and viewers are expected to understand that a photo has been altered and that that is how things work in the industry nowadays. But this isn't the case. The pressure hasn't lessened on girls to be thin or boys to be more muscular since we started becoming more aware of the falseness of photos. It doesn't seem to matter whether or not we understand that a photo has been altered, especially when real people are still held to those impossible expectations.

Out of dozens of magazines researched by *Street Cents*, only *Toro* and *CosmoGirl* give any sort of credit to photo retouching. Retoucher Glenn Feron told *Street Cents* that he has never been given credit for his work. To his knowledge, no magazine or ad has ever credited him and he does not expect to receive any accreditation anytime soon. Why is everything so hush-hush? Is it important that we don't directly see that a photo has been altered in order to keep up the illusion of beauty?

The Ethics of It All

With all these manipulations going on in photos, we began to wonder if anyone at all feels an ethical obligation toward this? Do retouchers care that their work affects the psyche and self-esteem of so many teens? Do the magazines that hire them and direct the manipulations feel any sort of responsibility?

None of the magazines that *Street Cents* spoke to have a retouching policy or any sort of written document that restricts the manipulations that can be done. However, all magazines interviewed said that they worked under a code of ethics that is not written down, but is upheld in-house, that keeps them from doing extreme manipulations such as swapping heads and bodies of different models and drastically altering the features and body shape of the models.

None of the retouchers that spoke with *Street Cents* felt any sort of ethical obligation with their work. They told us that they are paid to create beautiful images that the public should understand are altered. They say they are artists and should be recognized as such, because it is the fashion magazine industry and YOU, the consumer, that are dictating what is the acceptable image of beauty.

While retouching in the fashion world is a bit of a free-for-all, with no one regulating who does what and artists relying simply on their own code of ethics to monitor the industry, *Street Cents* was relieved to find out such is not the same for journalism.

VOL. 161, NO. 2   FEBRUARY 1982

NATIONAL GEOGRAPHIC

NAPOLEON 142

EGYPT'S DESERT OF PROMISE 190

HUMMINGBIRDS: THE NECTAR CONNECTION 223

TREASURE FROM THE GHOST GALLEON 228

NOMADS OF CHINA'S WEST 244

STRANGE WORLD OF PALAU'S SALT LAKES 264

SEE "EGYPT: QUEST FOR ETERNITY" WEDNESDAY, FEBRUARY 3, ON PBS TV

Photo retouching isn't just for people. *National Geographic* squeezed two pyramids together so they would fit on their 1983 cover.

Don't Go There!

There are no Canadian laws stopping magazines from retouching whatever they want, but there are MANY standards and professional codes of ethics making sure that our journalists aren't lying to us. There's a whole different set of standards that journalists have to follow in order to ensure that we are getting the truth. And while we expect what we read in our local paper is fact, recently photo journalism has come under fire.

> "Basically, we're selling a product—we're selling an image. To those who say too much retouching, I say you are bogus. This is the world that we're living in. Everything is glorified. I say live in your time."
>
> — Hollywood photo-retoucher, Pascal Dangin

In the March 6, 2005, issue of *Newsweek*, a composite photo of Martha Stewart's head and a model's body was used. The photo was clearly a fake because Martha was still in jail at the time of the magazine release. Due to the media and public outrage over the Martha cover, *Newsweek* now has bylines for cover photos and illustrations that appear directly on the cover. This new practice has made them the first major news magazine to adopt the crediting policy.

OK, so now you know a little or a lot more about retouching, but it's still hard, no matter what you know, not to stare longingly at the celebrity photos and wish you could look like them. But do your best to remember what Libertee Muzyka, formerly of *Stuff* and *Maxim* Online magazine told *Street Cents*—"I would love to have her abs, and guess what? So would she."

Check out this "ghost" special effect image by Jacques Henri Lartigue, taken in 1905. Since we first started taking photos, more than 100 years ago, we've been able to manipulate and alter an image. But only recently, with digital and computer technology, have we been able to do so much with so little.

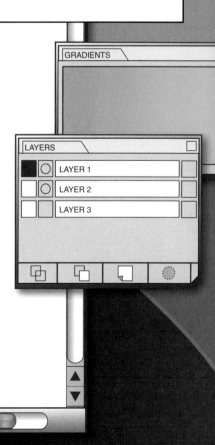

Reflecting

Synthesizing: This selection provides a variety of examples of photos being intentionally doctored. How do the photos help you better understand the text?

Metacognition: How did your thinking about altering photos change over the course of reading this selection? What particular points in the article caused that change?

Media Literacy: *Street Cents* is a program that talks to teens about a variety of media and pop culture issues. What point are the producers trying to make in this article? Do you agree with that point?

The Zoo

Short Story by Edward D. Hoch

The children were always good during the month of August, especially when it began to get near the twenty-third. It was on this day that the great silver spaceship carrying Professor Hugo's Interplanetary Zoo settled down for its annual six-hour visit to the Chicago area.

Before daybreak the crowds would form, long lines of children and adults both, each one clutching his or her dollar, and waiting with wonderment to see what race of strange creatures the professor had brought this year.

In the past they had been treated to three-legged creatures from Venus, or tall, thin men from Mars, or even snake-like horrors from somewhere more distant. This year, as the great round ship settled slowly to Earth in the huge tri-city parking area just outside of Chicago, they watched with awe as the sides slowly slid up to reveal the familiar barred cages. In them were some wild breed of nightmare— small, horse-like animals that moved with quick, jerking motions and constantly chattered in a high-pitched tongue. The citizens of Earth clustered around as Professor Hugo's crew quickly collected the waiting dollars, and soon the good professor himself made an appearance, wearing his many-coloured rainbow cape and top hat. "Peoples of Earth," he called into his microphone.

The crowd's noise died down and he continued. "Peoples of Earth, this year you see a real treat for your single dollar—the little-known horse-spider people of Kaan—brought to you across a million kilometres of space at great expense. Gather around, see them, study them, listen to them, tell your friends about them. But hurry! My ship can remain here only six hours!"

And the crowds slowly filed by, at once horrified and fascinated by these strange creatures that looked like horses but ran up the walls of their cages like spiders. "This is certainly worth a dollar," one man remarked, hurrying away. "I'm going home to get my wife."

All day long it went like that, until ten thousand people had filed by the barred cages set into the side of the spaceship. Then, as the six-hour limit ran out, Professor Hugo once more took the microphone in hand. "We must go now, but we will return next year on this date. And if you enjoyed our zoo this year, telephone your friends in other cities about it. We will land in New York tomorrow, and next week on to London, Paris, Rome, Hong Kong, and Tokyo. Then on to other worlds!"

He waved farewell to them, and as the ship rose from the ground, the Earth peoples agreed that this had been the very best Zoo yet....

Some two months and three planets later, the silver ship of Professor Hugo settled at last onto the familiar jagged rocks of Kaan, and the queer horse-spider creatures filed quickly out of their cages. Professor Hugo was there to say a few parting words, and then they scurried away in a hundred different directions, seeking their homes among the rocks.

In one house, the she-creature was happy to see the return of her mate and offspring. She babbled a greeting in the strange tongue and hurried to embrace them. "It was a long time you were gone. Was it good?"

And the he-creature nodded. "The little one enjoyed it especially. We visited eight worlds and saw many things."

The little one ran up the wall of the cave. "On the place called Earth it was the best. The creatures there wear garments over their skins, and they walk on two legs."

"But isn't it dangerous?" asked the she-creature.

"No," her mate answered. "There are bars to protect us from them. We remain right in the ship. Next time you must come with us. It is well worth the nineteen commocs it costs."

And the little one nodded. "It was the very best Zoo ever...."

Reflecting

Synthesizing: Part of synthesizing is comparing and contrasting a text to other texts you know. In what ways is this story like or unlike other articles or stories you've read about zoos? How does this selection connect to other selections you've read?

Metacognition: At what point in the story did you find the strategy of rereading most helpful? Explain how rereading enhanced your understanding.

Critical Literacy: This story tries to show you the perspective on either side of a zoo's barred cages, to make you think more critically about zoos. How effectively does it achieve that goal?

How to **Improve Fluency**

> Remember that varying your sentences can change the mood or pace of your writing. This writer has experimented to create two very different introductions.
>
> ### Sample 1
>
> Can this be real? How often had I asked myself that? Millions of times in the past year. What can you do, though, if you don't know the truth? Nothing! I had to take the photo at face value. Either it was a picture of my real parents or it wasn't.
>
> ### Sample 2
>
> The photo pinned to my bulletin board always made me shiver slightly. A simple photo, it showed two happy-looking people staring out at the camera, laughing. The background was blurred, so you couldn't tell where they stood. Could they really be my parents?

Fluent writing flows easily and engages your readers. One way to improve your fluency is to increase your sentence variety.

- ✓ **Use a combination of short and long sentences.** Short sentences require your readers to pick up their reading pace, say for an action scene. Long sentences require readers to slow down and think.

- ✓ **Vary the types of sentences you use** (statements, questions, and exclamations). Having lots of statements in a row may bore readers. Questions involve readers in the text. Short exclamations break up longer explanations.

- ✓ **Combine short sentences** into compound or complex sentences to make your writing less choppy.

- ✓ **Vary the beginnings of sentences**, so you don't have a long string of sentences beginning the same way.

- ✓ **Use transition words effectively** to bridge sentences. For example, *however, therefore, for example, on the other hand.* But, remember that too many transition words will confuse your readers or muddy the logical flow of ideas.

It's important to read your writing aloud in order to check that it's fluent. Ask yourself: How does this section sound? Do my ideas flow naturally from line to line? Have I used transitions to connect ideas logically?

Transfer Your Learning

Across the Strands

Reading: When you read a text that isn't fluent, how does it affect your enjoyment of the text?

Across the Curriculum

History: Historical texts often contain complex, detailed information. How can writers of these texts make their writing fluent?

Talk About It
Would you call reality TV *real*? Why or why not?

How Reality TV Fakes It

The Truth About Reality TV
Editorial by Carmen Li, *The West Coast Times*

Would it shock you to know that "reality TV" isn't real? Okay, so you probably know that the situations on reality shows are manipulated, but you might be surprised to find out how much. And now, thanks to a dispute between the producers and freelance consultants who work on these shows, secrets are being spilled.

In recent weeks, a number of reality TV consultants have spoken out, exposing the tricks reality shows use. It's been revealed, for instance, that events are restaged if cameras don't capture an event or conversation the first time it happens. Audio and video from different times are combined to make it look like participants are doing something they're not. Episodes are planned before taping. Crushes and feuds are constructed or manipulated by producers, and quotes are manufactured.

Fluency

Fluent writers use transition words to bridge sentences and show the flow of ideas. How does the transition phrase in this paragraph help you follow the idea being presented?

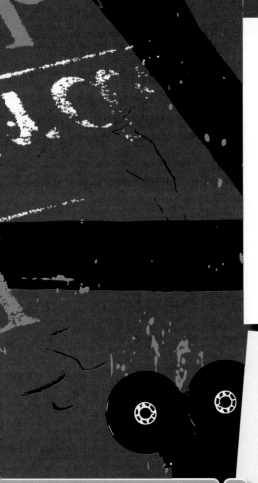

Jeff Bartsch, a freelance editor who has worked on several reality shows, talks about how it's common to feature actors in the roles of supposedly real people: "Producers have to do this sometimes because they're looking for a specific type of person to fit a role."

Producers say viewers know these shows aren't real, and viewers don't care. In addition, the producers claim that reality TV isn't about being real, it's about being interesting. Mark Burnett, a producer of some of the most popular reality shows says, "I tell good stories. It really is not reality TV. It really is unscripted drama."

A complicated issue to be sure. What do you think?

Letters to the Editor

Dear Editor,

Thank you for publishing the article "The Truth About Reality TV." This article confirms what I have thought for a very long time now. Reality TV is a curse. It is ruining our society and destroying our ability to think. What are we doing to ourselves by allowing this trash on our TV screens?

Our society suffers when people stop living their lives because they'd rather watch the lives of complete strangers on TV. Why exercise, play a sport, volunteer, or read a newspaper when you can watch people on TV argue? Today, people can't carry on a conversation without mentioning what happened last night on some ridiculous show. Our obsession with reality TV means real issues are being ignored. Global concerns are being ignored. Families and friends are being ignored!

To make matters worse, these "reality" shows aren't even real. Don't people feel angry knowing they've been lied to?! If someone tried to trick me, if someone treated me like I was an idiot, I'd be mad! There is some great TV out there written by talented writers and acted by skilled actors. These are the shows that deserve ratings. Stop letting rich producers make fools of you! Stop wasting your time on lies! Change the channel!

Thank you for your time,
Alex Varade, Gander, Newfoundland

Fluency

→

Fluent writers vary the types of sentences they use and combine short sentences into compound or complex sentences. Why might the writer use a very short sentence here?

Fluency

→

Fluent writers use a combination of short and long sentences. Notice how this writer changes his pace by changing from long to short sentences. How does that affect his readers?

Hello there,

Your article "The Truth About Reality TV" really got me thinking. I hear it a lot lately: Reality TV is horrible. It's fake and it's cheap. It's senseless, meaningless, and dumb. My question is: If this is true, why are so many people watching it?

I watch reality TV. I think it's valuable. Why? First of all, it's really entertaining and cheap! I can see great comedians, dancers, and singers without paying $40 for concert tickets. I can watch shows that make me laugh, cry, and think.

If you feel tricked because you find out lines are scripted—well, deal with it! Move on! Knowing that some of the reality is fake shouldn't stop you from enjoying the drama!

As well, reality TV doesn't just entertain, it educates. That's right! I think we *do* learn something when we watch reality TV. Because when we watch these shows, we contemplate our own behaviour. I watch it and realize I would never cry because my housemate ate my cookie. I would never compete for a date. I would totally know to plug my nose so I could eat 12 hissing cockroaches.

Sure, it's addictive. It's also totally healthy! Watching other people is human nature. Reality TV gives us entertainment, hilarity, and horror, all while providing us with valuable insight. So let's all just finally admit it. Come on, say it with me: "I watch reality TV."

Christine Belzer, Aberdeen, Saskatchewan

← Fluency

Fluent writers vary the beginnings of sentences. Imagine how this paragraph would sound if the writer had started each of these sentences with "Reality TV is...."

Reflecting

Reading Like a Writer: Read the letters aloud and consider their pace and how they sound. In your opinion, which aspects of fluency have the writers used most effectively?

Metacognition: When you assess how fluent your own writing is, what helps you spot and correct any problems?

Synthesizing: How does reading a magazine article and two letters with differing viewpoints help you understand the issue of reality TV? How did your response to the issue change as you read each piece?

MY POCKETS AIN'T THAT PHAT

Poem by Shysuaune T. Taylor

I
rotate to the rhythm
   of a ghetto
      grape
      jimbe
      voice
my step
is faaaaarrr to the left
and I don't
wanna keep up
     with Generation
     X-pense
     X-plore
     X-cite
     X-press myself
my groove clues of
reds, blacks, and blues
I don't
    wear nothing
of a
Nautica
Eddie Bauer
   Nike
   Fila
   Timbo-
   Land

      Rockport
      Mike Jordan
      Scent
My clothes
       stay big
       Kmart cool
       Target fresh
I'm not a
hip hop
Dred
Retro
       4-pierced brotha
Don't wanna be wrapped
up in ' 70s leather
polyester Afro zones
My hair is
    Not
    tightly faded
    brown-skinned
    flawless, suave
My ride ain't
      a drop top
      bassed
      hydraulic
      screamin'
      bling wagon

I'm cream
    Neutral
    Chills
of grey brown patterns
Forgive me for not
speaking.
        My dance of rejection
        freaks me breathless.
In a room of
        human collages
I'd rather sit and converse
with anger, happiness,
        my personality's
        offspring
I'm not
down with impressing
        anyone's impression
of an urban hip hop image
No, that stereotype
        doesn't move me
My words
        complement those
          that welcome them.
'Til then they stay
colourfully quiet with
a lot of
a little to
say!

At the time he wrote this, Shysuaune was 18.

Poets' Message Board

Love the arrangement of the lines. So good. The words fall down the page, like water. Nice flow. Great Poem.

—kat

Ummm, yeah. I'm not sure I get this poem. I'm gonna be honest, I think the poet's trying 2 hard 2 be cool.

—sir davis hilton

Maybe the poet just IS cool. The thing is, it's impossible to tell. That's the beauty of poetry; every poem shouldn't be for everyone. It's personal expression. A poem is like meeting someone in person. You meet some people and just get them. You meet other people and just don't.

—kat

Well, I don't know if I'd get this guy then. Why put a word on every line? How do you read this poem? What's jimbe?

—sir davis hilton

Jimbe is a reference to an African drum. Don't stress over every word. I am feelin' this one. It's sayin' be original.

—chris

Reflecting

Reading Like a Writer: Read the message board and consider how each speaker uses sentence variety to create fluency. Choose one message and think about what transition words would help to improve the flow of ideas.

Metacognition: What strategies did you use to make sense of this poem?

Critical Literacy: Why do you think the poet wrote this poem? Who did he write it for? Who might object to his message?

Talk About It
What medium (painting, song, movie, and so on) would you use to communicate who you are?

Partridge Poems

Magazine Profile by Anna Leventhal

Taqralik Partridge is a spoken-word artist who didn't see her reality depicted in today's popular culture. So she put it there herself.

Today, Taqralik Partridge is using her performances as a way to express pride in her culture and educate audiences about Inuit people.

Taqralik's writing is defined by her ability to tell stories deeply rooted in the rich dirt of everyday life. Her subjects aren't mythical heroes or goddesses: the world they live in is both ordinary and highly charged. Her piece "Eskimo Chick" is both a heartfelt tribute to a friend and a sly poke at the clichés of girl culture. "Other girls have Louis Vuitton baggage and Calvin Klein pasts," she chuckles in her performance, "but you and me, we got sealskin hopes and dreams."

The child of an Inuk father and a white mother, Taqralik was raised in Kuujjuaq, a village in northern Québec. "Because I grew up in the North, I identify more with being Inuk. But I never had an Inuk woman in the house," she says. "I feel like everything about Inuit women fascinates me because there's that little bit of otherness, and they're also me at the same time."

Now living in Montréal, Taqralik can also attest to the tensions of life as an urban Inuk. "I've lived in the South for 12 years but I've always felt like an outsider," she says. "It's very strange to me how we can live and have two realities. I come from this place that's vast and open and beautiful, but I live and work in this place that is constricted and full of so many things going on. I love Montréal and I love the city, and [yet] in many ways I feel like an outsider."

Her work refuses to choose one reality over another. She skims from choppy rhymes to barely breathed stories that are almost lullabies, then suddenly she'll switch to traditional Inuit throat singing. She isn't merging two worlds so much as keeping them in constant conversation.

Taqralik has been writing all her life, but after she heard spoken-word artist Ian Kamau perform on K-OS's track "Papercuts," she finally had a name for what she wanted to do. "I heard this guy come on doing something that was sort of like rap, but not, and it totally seized me," she says. "I Googled him and found out it was called *spoken word*, and I knew that was something I wanted to do."

Since then, Taqralik has performed for a range of audiences. Sometimes she takes the stage with a DJ or her newly formed band, Descendants. Sometimes it's just her voice and a microphone.

We are thick in blood
we are thick in blood
our family tree
is really
rivers
branching out over
thousands of miles

Spoken word—the style of performance poetry where the rhythm of the piece carries the words—is associated with hip cafés, not remote settlements with teenagers in pickup trucks hanging out in parking lots. There was a time when even hip hop was entirely foreign to kids who, like Taqralik, grew up in rural northern villages.

"In the North, before the Internet, we didn't have access to that kind of music. I didn't grow up listening to hip hop—I grew up listening to Johnny Cash and Iron Maiden," she laughs. But Taqralik makes the style work for her, negotiating the rocky terrain of rhythm and words. It would be a stretch to call her an MC—her pieces are slower, more lyrical, and less beat-oriented. But she credits positive hip hop for her inspiration. "The whole idea of people being downtrodden and having to get up and do something with themselves really appeals to me," she says.

Writers often talk about the importance of listening to their inner voice. "I was so worried for a long time about writing about where I come from," Taqralik says. "First of all, I thought that I didn't have much to say or that I wasn't the right person to say it; all these excuses of why I wouldn't be good enough."

As a teenager, Taqralik wrote self-described bad poetry, the memory of which makes her shudder. She was just an ordinary kid from Kuujjuaq with everyday worries and hopes. But what she calls "an unstoppable urge to write" finally made her confront her demons and start producing serious work.

Taqralik doesn't shrink from heavy subjects like violence or poverty. To her, they're as much a part of reality as rush-hour traffic or big mitts in the winter, and just as important to talk about. But sometimes the line between the personal and the universal gets blurry. "At first when I was writing I thought, 'I'll never show this to Inuit, because someone's going to think it's about her,'" she says.

Taqralik's stories don't plaster over the grittier side of the life she knows, and they don't romanticize or pity their subjects. "I see Inuit women who are professionals, who have big fancy jobs," she explains, "and then others who have social problems, or they're dirt poor, but they're good storytellers. It's just a big mess that I love. It doesn't really matter what her social status is or what successes she's had, materially. I'm just totally in awe of Inuit women."

A new generation is in awe of Taqralik. She's showing teens of both genders that pop culture is what you make it.

Reflecting

Reading Like a Writer: In this selection you hear two fluent voices: the first voice is the writer of the profile, Anna Leventhal; the second voice appears in the quotations Taqralik Partridge gives Anna. How does using quotations change the pace or mood of the article?

Metacognition: What did you learn from this selection about improving fluency that you would like to try in your own writing?

Synthesizing: How do the quotations in this profile add to your understanding of Taqralik Partridge?

How to ▷ Synthesize While Listening

Active listeners synthesize oral texts to gain new understanding. You synthesize by combining what you know with what you're hearing, to come up with a new understanding or to form an opinion.

Use these strategies to synthesize while listening.	For example, you're listening to a radio interview with a dancer speaking about his training—and you've never danced before.
Connect what you are hearing with your personal experiences. Connections can help you make sense of new information.	You may not personally connect with the specific exercises and workout schedule that the dancer describes. However, you can draw on your experience with training for another sport, such as hockey.
Compare what you are hearing with what you have read or heard in other texts. Reflecting on similarities can help you make connections.	You may see similarities between the training the dancer describes and what you've read about the training of other athletes.
Contrast what you are hearing with what you already know or believe. Assess information that is new or that challenges what you believe to be true. A focus on differences helps you form new opinions.	If the speaker says, "With the right training and practice, anyone can be an excellent dancer," you might question this because you know that some sports require a skill that not everyone has.

When you listen to difficult texts, the Connect-Compare-Contrast strategies will help you organize your thoughts and gain a new understanding. After listening, ask yourself: How has my thinking changed? What do I understand now that I didn't understand before?

Transfer Your Learning

Across the Strands

Media Literacy: Synthesizing while you listen can help you assess and analyze media texts like TV shows and movies. How will the visuals in these formats help you synthesize?

Across the Curriculum

Science and Technology: How might the synthesizing strategies (connect, compare, and contrast) help you when you're listening to someone describe the melting of Arctic ice shelves?

UNDERSTANDING LISTENING STRATEGIES

▶ Synthesizing While Listening

Talk About It
What do you think the title "Practically Twins" means?

Practically Twins

Script by Peg Kehret

In this script, the two actors are not speaking with each other, but to the audience. Their voices can overlap. Actors could be seated close together on the stage with their backs to one another.

Characters: Eleanor, Natasha—best friends
Setting: anywhere

ELEANOR: This is my friend, Natasha.

NATASHA: Who am I, really?

ELEANOR: Natasha is a gymnast. She does the uneven parallel bars.

Synthesizing While Listening

Listeners synthesize by connecting to their personal experiences. What connection do you make at this point? As you continue, make connections to increase your understanding of the characters and their problems. How do your connections help you understand the message and theme of the script?

NATASHA: I enjoy gymnastics, but it is not enough to say I am a gymnast. That is such a small part of me.

ELEANOR: She gets first place in practically every gymnastics meet. Our coach thinks she has Olympic potential.

NATASHA: My friend, Eleanor, likes to tell people that my coach thinks I have potential to make the Olympic squad someday. I wish she wouldn't always say that. I want her to like me for who I am, not for how I perform on the bars.

ELEANOR: Natasha and I have been friends since third grade. We live just two doors apart.

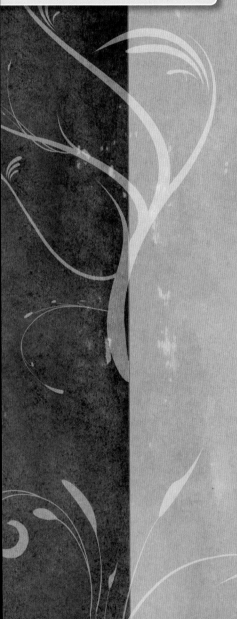

Synthesizing While Listening

Listeners compare what they are hearing to other texts they've heard or read. They reflect on similarities to make connections. What other stories or texts do you know where someone was confused about what they wanted? How does making that connection help you understand Natasha?

NATASHA: In the third grade, I knew who I was and I knew what I wanted to do with my life. I wanted to be a mail carrier. I loved to get mail. I thought it would be wonderful to be a mail carrier and bring excitement and joy to the people on my route. Later, when I learned that mail carriers also bring bills and ads, I lost my enthusiasm. The trouble is, I haven't replaced that enthusiasm with a new goal. What do I want to be? What can I do with my life?

ELEANOR: Imagine being good enough to make the Olympics!

NATASHA: Sometimes I get so tired of practising my routines. People don't realize how many hours of hard work it takes to be good at a sport. And you have to do it every day. No exceptions. But whenever I think of quitting, I can't. If I quit, I'd never know whether I would have made it or not.

ELEANOR: Natasha's parents are both doctors. No wonder she's so smart. No wonder she never gets sick. I'm always getting a cold or the chicken pox or a touch of the flu, but Natasha is as strong as an elephant.

NATASHA: People are too impressed with doctors. The minute anyone finds out that my parents are doctors they make three assumptions: 1. We're rich. 2. My parents are brilliant. 3. I'll be a doctor someday, too.

ELEANOR: I suppose Natasha will go to medical school eventually, but I hope she trains for the Olympics first.

NATASHA: I have no desire to be a doctor. For most families, dinner table conversation is about sports or current events or what happened in school. My family discusses the complications of gallbladder surgery or so-and-so's white blood count or patient X's liver disease. It isn't very appetizing.

ELEANOR: Except for her parents being doctors and her being so good at gymnastics, Natasha and I are pretty much the same. I feel so blessed to have a friend like Natasha. I hope that we'll always be this close. We go to the same school and have the same friends. We're practically twins.

NATASHA: Eleanor has a whole circle of friends. I'm included in all their activities, but they aren't really my friends. They're acquaintances. I like everyone in our group, but I never think the way they do. I always feel different, like I don't quite fit in.

ELEANOR: If Natasha ever moved away, I think I'd die of loneliness. I tell her everything—and she tells me everything. The amazing thing is, we always agree.

NATASHA: It's lonely to feel different. Eleanor's lucky. She'll go through life happy, doing what's expected of her, never challenging the rules. It must feel comfortable to just accept things as they are and never hunger for more.

ELEANOR: Natasha's lucky. It must be wonderful to be smart and talented. I'm ordinary; my life is predictable. I'll probably get a job in this small town right after high school. Not that there's anything wrong with that, but it means I may live my whole life right here, within shouting distance of where I started kindergarten.

NATASHA: When I think of all the options, it's scary. I want to see other countries, learn other languages, experience other thinking. I want to stretch my mind.

ELEANOR: There won't ever be any extraordinary excitement in my life. My thrills will have to come through knowing people like Natasha.

NATASHA: Life was easier when all I wanted was to deliver the mail.

ELEANOR: I wish I could be on the Olympic team.

Synthesizing While Listening

Listeners contrast what they are hearing with what they already know or believe. Each character values something different. How does contrasting what they value with your own values help you respond to the selection?

Reflecting

Synthesizing While Listening: After the first few lines of the script, what did you think about each character? What new understanding of the characters did you have by the end of the script? How did your thinking about the characters change?

Metacognition: What helped you to synthesize most effectively in this script—connecting, comparing, or contrasting? Explain your response.

Critical Literacy: What does the writer of this script seem to value? Support your answer with evidence from the text.

Talk About It

What would you do if you signed a million dollar recording contract?

SO YOU WANT TO BE A MUSIC STAR?

Radio Transcript by Alan Cross

As a musician, there are three ways that you can go about conducting business in the music industry.

Method number one involves doing everything yourself. You write the songs; book the studio time; produce the music; deliver your CDs to record stores; track sales; book your tours; print your T-shirts; design and maintain your websites; take care of publicity; finance your video; oversee marketing, licensing, and publishing—and then hope for the best.

You'll never sleep, but at least you'll have control over every aspect of your career. You are an independent recording artist. And, most likely, you're a starving artist, because all these expenses come out of your pocket.

The second method involves signing a deal with an independent record label. You still do almost everything yourself, but at least there are some people in an office working on the business side of things for you.

A third route involves signing with one of the four major multinational record labels. Once you sign on the dotted line, they take care of all the business stuff. The theory is that the label will take care of your business matters while you concentrate on the music.

This is the big time. If you sign with a major label, you've hit pay dirt, right? Isn't a major deal supposed to make you rich and famous? Well, no.

Let's say you're in a hot young four-piece band that signs with a major record label. They give you a 20 percent royalty rate and a million-dollar advance.

A million bucks! You're rich! Or are you?

Actually, that million dollars is just a loan from the record company. It needs to be repaid from any profits that you might earn in the future. In other words, you start your major label recording career one million dollars in debt. Where does the money go?

Let's say half a million goes to recording your debut album. Suddenly, you're down to $500 000. Then, you have to pay your lawyer, accountant, business manager, road manager, and road crew. Those costs total $150 000. Now there are taxes to be paid, which could be as high as 50 percent. When the dust clears, there's just $175 000 left for four band members to split. That equals about $44 000 per member, and that's what everyone has to live on until the record is released.

Still, $44 000 sounds like a decent amount of cake for anyone in a young band, right? But, out of that, you have to pay your rent and buy clothes, food, and any new equipment you might need—and there's no more money coming until the album is released. When will that be?

That's at the discretion of the record label. It might be right away, but they have the right to sit on it for a year … or two … or longer. They may send it back for rewriting, re-recording, and/or remixing. Or, they might just wait until the market cycle is in a place where the record has a better chance of succeeding.

Finally, the record comes out. It's a big hit and sells a million copies. Two singles are taken from the album and each single is accompanied by a video. The cost of making each videos is $500 000. The label only pays for half of that, so you're in debt another $500 000. Then you have to go on tour to promote your album. That costs money, as does promoting the tour, so now you're in debt another $500 000.

That million-dollar record deal has quickly turned into a $2 million debt. And we're not done yet.

Remember: You sold one million copies of your album and your royalty rate is 20 percent. If we say that means $2 per CD, you've just earned $2 million! But that $2 million minus your $2 million debt equals $0. All that work, all that effort, and all that success, and you've made exactly nothing.

Meanwhile, your major label hasn't made a lot of money, either. From the beginning, it's been in their best interest to make you as big a star as possible. They spend millions of dollars paying for new artists' CDs and tours. And the majority of these artists—literally 20 out of 30 newly signed artists—never make that money back.

It's a tough way to make a living on both sides of the artist/label equation.

Reflecting

Synthesizing: At the beginning of this selection, what was your opinion about artists working with major label recording contracts? Did your opinion change? If so, how?

Metacognition: What synthesizing strategies (connect, compare, and contrast) helped you form an opinion in response to this selection?

How to ▶ Analyze Media Elements

Media texts are designed to tell a certain story or send a certain message. The message a media text sends to its audience is made more powerful when different media elements are used and combined effectively.

As time goes by, we become more familiar with the elements in media texts. As a result, these texts can lose their ability to catch our eye. To combat this, producers create media texts that use elements in surprising or different ways. Looking carefully at and questioning the purpose of these elements is the best way to understand a media text's true message.

If you're looking for a sports magazine, what makes you pick one up over the others? The title treatment, the colours, the photos, and the text have all been combined with a particular audience in mind. These elements work together so powerfully that your eye goes straight to the magazine.

For example, consider the media elements in reusable shopping bags. They tell an audience that the store selling them is concerned with the environment. How do the elements do that? Why would that message be important?

company logo

company brand

colour—green, to reflect environmental message

text in English and French

image—bottle image used because bag is made from recycled plastic bottles

text—reflects environmental message

Some Questions to Ask As You Analyze Media Elements

- What is the form of this media text?

- What media elements does this form usually use?

- Is this media text using elements in a way that is new, unusual, or surprising?

- Why has this media text used these specific media elements? What message does that send?

- How do these elements support my understanding of this media text?

- How effectively are the media elements used?

- What media elements make this media text powerful (or not)?

- How are the elements of the media text combined to create or enhance meaning?

Media forms include songs, newspapers, magazines, movies, TV shows, maps, shopping bags, running shoes, posters, radio commercials, T-shirts, and so on.

The media elements used in different forms can vary greatly. Print ad elements, for example, include slogans, words, visuals, colour, logos, costumes, sets, different camera angles, and so on. In TV commercials, the usual media elements also include music, sound effects, dialogue, voice-overs, different types of shots (such as close-ups, crane shots), and so on.

Here's another example of a shopping bag with a message. How effectively is it using the elements listed on the previous page?

Transfer Your Learning

Across the Strands

Reading: What did you learn about synthesizing while reading that can help you analyze the use of elements in a media text?

Across the Curriculum

History: If you were asked to create a print ad to promote immigration to Canada, how would you use the usual media elements of an ad to surprise your audience?

Building Buzz

Teaser and Viral Ads from various sources

Hey, You, Pay Attention!

Teaser ads are designed to tease the public by offering only bits of information without revealing either the sponsor of the ad or the product being advertised. Teaser ads are the front-runners of an advertising campaign, and their purpose is to arouse curiosity and get attention for the campaign that follows. Teaser ads use elements that are very similar to the elements in regular advertising.

Analyzing Media Elements →

Begin by identifying the media form. This selection features posters used in an advertising campaign. What are the makers of this ad trying to sell? Is there anything that strikes you as unusual?

Our teenagers don't have their own goals anymore.

Obay™ works like a charm.

From the makers of WhyBecauseISaidSo.™

← **Analyzing Media Elements**

Identify the elements that the media text uses. How are the elements of teaser ads similar to those of regular ads? How are they different?

Now That We Have Your Attention

Teaser ads feature an element not used in regular ad campaigns: the reveal. The reveal is the second half of the advertising campaign and it tells the audience what the ads are about. The Obay campaign uses a fairly simple reveal—a yellow note over the original image.

← **Analyzing Media Elements**

Identify the purpose of the media elements. Consider how those elements support your understanding of the media text. What purpose does the reveal serve? How does the reveal help you understand the original teaser ads?

© 2003 P&G

Analyzing Media Elements →

Identify the media elements that make the media text enjoyable or powerful. What elements in this teaser ad might make a viewer stop and take notice of it?

Simple or Complex

Reveal ads can be simple or complex. In this Mr. Clean reveal, the audience is shown the poster, plus the bus shelter cleaned up, repaired, and painted. All of these elements contribute to the advertiser's message.

Analyzing Media Elements →

Reflect on how media elements are combined to enhance meaning. How do all of the elements in this ad campaign enhance its message? What message is this ad campaign sending?

Politics, Prejudice, Pollution.

Fight the dirty stuff.

Mr. Clean

2004 Global VPI • 102,000,000 Points

Look Over HERE!

As we've seen in the previous examples, media elements used in unusual or new ways can have a powerful effect on a viewer. Using a minimal number of media elements can also have a striking effect. Consider these teaser movie posters. In order for these ads to be successful, people have to care enough to wonder what they mean. Think about what isn't in these ads. How do the missing elements add to the power of the ad? Teaser movie ads also create interest by only hinting at what a movie might be about. If you look closely though, the details can tell you quite a bit.

Reflecting

Media Literacy: Which of these advertising campaigns do you think is the most effective? Support your response with evidence from the selection.

Metacognition: What strategies did you use to help you analyze the elements of these ads?

Connecting to Other Media: How would you change one of these ad campaigns, and its elements, to make it suitable for radio or TV?

Talk About It

What usual elements do successful radio ads use to catch your attention?

DECODING RADIO

Radio Ads from various sources

Big Mike's Exotic Animal Sanctuary

BIG MIKE: Hi, Mike here, from Big Mike's Exotic Animal Sanctuary, where your family can see lions up close.

Cue cat meow.

BIG MIKE: Well, they're not really lions, they're just cats shaved to look like lions.

Cue higher-pitched meow of a small cat.

BIG MIKE: But you can pat these lions. Yeah.

Cue the howl of an angry cat and a crash.

BIG MIKE: Ow! Well, not that one. And we have lots of brown and black bears.

Cue dog barking.

BIG MIKE: And we have some zebras too.

Cue horse whinnying.

BIG MIKE: Unless it rains. And then they're just kinda horses.

ANNOUNCER: There's no substitute for the zoo. Get your annual pass at the Calgary Zoo.

Hickory Dickory Dock

Interior scene, dining room. Sound FX: clink of cutlery on plate, ticking of large grandfather clock. Music throughout to tune of "Hickory Dickory Dock."

SQUEAKY VOICE: Psst. Over here. No, down here, that's right, here! Beside the clock.

Sound FX: chair scraping backward on wooden floor, glass, plate, cutlery crashing to floor.

MAN (SCREAMING): MOUSE!

Sound FX: crashing of furniture as if table and chairs are being overturned.

MAN (SCREAMING): MOUSE! MOUSE!

MOUSE (SQUEAKY VOICE): Wow! Not so loud, fella!

MAN (QUIETER, BUT STUTTERING): T-t-talking m-m-mouse!

MOUSE: What'd you expect? You've been feeding me **Cheese-Bits**, the 100% organic dairy product with added DHA! **Cheese-Bits**— available in three delicious flavours!

MAN: Wh-wh-what?!

MOUSE: You know, **Cheese-Bits** with DHA—docosahexaenoic acid—it's an omega-3 essential fatty acid that helps promote the growth of phospholipids in the brain and retinas. Not only have **Cheese-Bits** made me smarter and given me better eyesight, they've helped cure my ADHD—you know: Attention Deficit Hyperactivity Disorder. I'm not running up that stupid clock anymore! As well, **Cheese-Bits** have limited the risk of my getting Alzheimer's disease. Plus I'm no longer depressed! Not even your stupid traps get me down anymore.

MAN: M-m-mouse t-t-talking!

MOUSE: Dude, you're not eating your **Cheese-Bits**!

Sound FX: scampering of little mice feet over wooden floor, crashing of chair, ticking of clock returns

ANNOUNCER: Dudes, eat your **Cheese-Bits**! Available everywhere fine foods are sold!

Reflecting

Analyzing Media: The two radio ads in this selection use their media elements in very different ways. What effect do these elements have on you?

Metacognition: At what point in the radio ads did you reflect and do a "reality check" to understand what the ads were about? What prompted your reflection?

Connecting to Other Media: How effective would these ads be if produced in a similar way for TV? What changes would have to be made to the dialogue or other elements?

Cause and Effect

When writers want to explain why things happen, they use a cause-and-effect text pattern. The cause is what happens first, and the effect is what happens as a result. A simple example is, if you forget to do your homework (the cause), then you may do poorly on the test (the effect).

More complicated examples may show how one cause can have more than one effect, or how one effect can have more than one cause. Think about another cause or effect that could be added to the simple example above.

One cause may result in a chain or series of effects. One of these may be the most important or noteworthy effect. Remember that different writers may choose to focus on one effect as being more important than another—depending on their perspective. In the example below, different writers might focus on different effects as being the most important.

> To identify and understand cause-and-effect text pattern, ask yourself: What happened first? What happened next? Why did that happen? How were the events connected? What was the most important effect?
>
> As well, look for key phrases: *if ... then, as a result, this led to, consequently, unless, for this reason, that's why, since, therefore.*

Cause	Effect	Effect	Effect
Canadian railroad is completed	goods travel back and forth more easily	people settle in the Western provinces	the way of life for First Nations peoples changes drastically

Transfer Your Learning

Across the Strands

Oral Communication: Think about the last conversation you had that used any of the key phrases listed above. What causes and effects were the focus of the conversation?

Across the Curriculum

Health: Health articles are often about the consequences of doing or not doing something. For example, an article about exercising might use this pattern. What do you think the cause(s) and effect(s) would be in such an article?

Talk About It

Do brand-name sneakers make a difference to your athletic performance?

Starbury Says "Enough"

News Report by John Stossel and Frank Mastropolo

Starbury 1s: Did these sneakers start a revolution?

Cause-and-Effect Text Pattern

Cause-and-effect text pattern explains why things happen. After reading the title and first two paragraphs, what cause(s) and effect(s) might be explored in the rest of the article?

One NBA Star Says Fashion Doesn't Have to Hurt Your Wallet

Sneakers today are a hot fashion item. Hip-hop stars rap about their Nikes in songs like "Air Force Ones," named after Nike's bestseller. Kids get robbed for their sneakers, or worse—some have even been killed.

So, how did the simple sneaker change from a canvas and rubber thing that allows you to run in comfort to today's $100-plus high fashion statement?

The Air Jordan

It began 20 years ago when Nike signed basketball superstar Michael Jordan as a spokesperson and then hired movie director Spike Lee to make a series of commercials for Nike's Air Jordan line. The ads popularized the catchphrase, "Money, it's gotta be the shoes!"

And this led to a world where many people believe "the shoes" help stars like Michael Jordan play so well. Many people consider $100-plus sneakers, even $200 sneakers, a necessity.

Cause-and-Effect Text Pattern

One effect can have several causes. What caused expensive sneakers to become popular?

"Suddenly sneakers became a status symbol, when in the past, they were just completely utilitarian [useful] things to put on your feet when you ran around the street," said Stuart Elliott, advertising columnist of *The New York Times*. "Nike came along and began to sell sneakers in a completely different way, through talking about fashion, and the idea that the sneaker helped you run faster or jump higher began to allow them to charge more for it."

Nike and other brands have made millions. Now Nike even has stores that sell $2000 sneakers, made of anaconda snake or crocodile with 18-karat gold accessories.

Starbury Had Enough

Enter Stephon Marbury, the NBA star of the New York Knicks, often called Starbury. He grew up poor, in a housing project in New York City. Stephon, one of seven children, wanted Air Jordans as a kid but for his mother, he says, that was an automatic "no."

"She just wasn't spending that type of money for sneakers," Stephon said. But he had to beg for those sneakers, "Because it was just the shoe to have. It was a fashion statement."

"Two hundred dollars was $200. It was a lot of money. It was a sacrifice," said Mabel Marbury, Stephon's mother. "Anybody that would take their money and buy a pair of sneakers and don't have no food in their house—is silly."

Stephon Marbury giving away his running shoes in New York City on *Starbury Give Back Day*

Starburys in stock

"The sneakers don't cost $100 to make. If you don't know that and you don't understand that, it's hard for you to grasp how much the shoe costs. It costs less than $14.98 to make a $150 shoe. That's not what people are being told."
— **Stephon Marbury**

Do the shoes make Marbury fly?

So when Stephon became Starbury, earning $17 million a year, he said "enough"; he would come out with a line of sneakers that sell for less than $15. He teamed with Steve & Barry's University Sportswear, an American chain store, and came out with the *Starbury* line of sneakers, hats, and jerseys. Nothing sells for more than $14.98.

"I think Stephon's own involvement is probably key here," said Michael Atmore, editorial director of *Footwear News*. "There's never been a big name athlete that's come out and said you don't need to pay as much. And that's what Stephon did."

Stephon made a 40-city tour when the sneakers debuted and Michael Atmore credits that for the shoe's success. "He showed the customer that he was behind it. And I think that's critical."

← **Cause-and-Effect Text Pattern**

One cause can have several effects. What effects resulted from Stephon, as a child, wanting sneakers that he and his family couldn't afford?

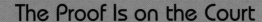

The Proof Is on the Court

Stephon wears the same sneakers on the basketball court that are sold in stores—proof, Stephon said, that he believes in their quality.

The result? In city after city, kids and parents rushed in. Andy Todd, president of Steve & Barry's, told ABC News that the chain sold out two months' inventory just three days after the sneakers debuted.

"Starbury, he thought about the kids. He thought about who can afford the Jordans," said one teen at Steve & Barry's. "So he put his sneakers to be $15, cheap, so other kids could buy sneakers."

What the Shoes Can Do

Stephon has won a new fan for his sneakers: Mark Cuban, owner of the NBA rival Dallas Mavericks. Mark was seen wearing a pair of Starburys at a Knicks–Mavericks game, and according to one basketball website, Mark said, "I love, love, love them. Are there better shoes? Yeah. Are there better shoes worth $120 dollars? No. I give him [Stephon] his credit. I don't think he has gotten enough props."

Mark went on to say, "There aren't many things we will do in our lives that will have an impact on culture and social change. To be able to send a message to people and sell millions of shoes, so the message gets through, saying, save that extra $85 and buy a guitar or some clothes. That is huge. You can look at 'NBA Cares' all you want. You can look at the things I've done for charity all you want. The NBA has never done anything as impactful as what [Stephon] has done."

"The shoes ain't going to make you jump higher," Stephon says of expensive shoes. "It's definitely not going to make you run faster. It does nothing but say that you got $150 pair of shoes on, that's it."

Cause-and-Effect Text Pattern

One cause may result in a chain or series of effects. One of these may be the most important or noteworthy effect. In this article, which do you think is the most important or noteworthy effect? Why?

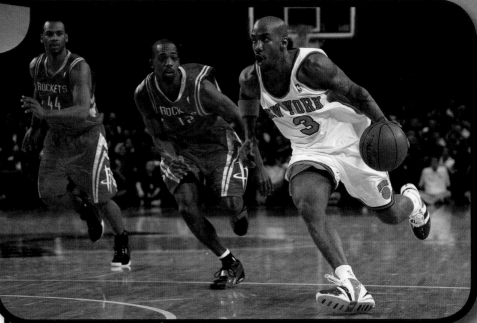

Starbury sneakers take on the more expensive brands.

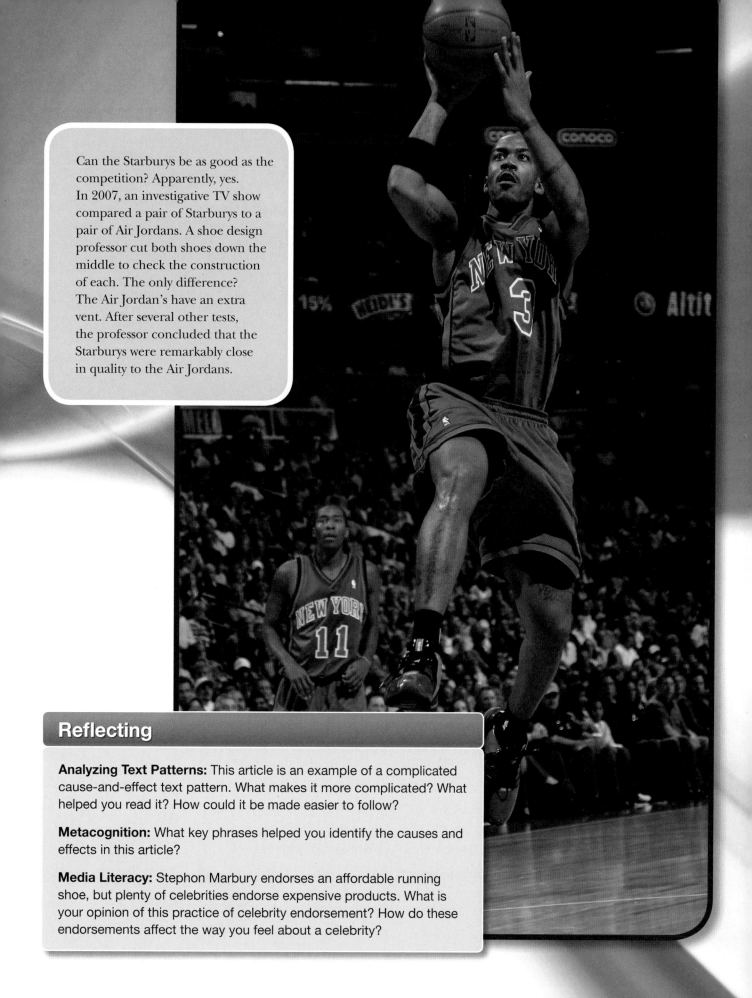

Can the Starburys be as good as the competition? Apparently, yes. In 2007, an investigative TV show compared a pair of Starburys to a pair of Air Jordans. A shoe design professor cut both shoes down the middle to check the construction of each. The only difference? The Air Jordan's have an extra vent. After several other tests, the professor concluded that the Starburys were remarkably close in quality to the Air Jordans.

Reflecting

Analyzing Text Patterns: This article is an example of a complicated cause-and-effect text pattern. What makes it more complicated? What helped you read it? How could it be made easier to follow?

Metacognition: What key phrases helped you identify the causes and effects in this article?

Media Literacy: Stephon Marbury endorses an affordable running shoe, but plenty of celebrities endorse expensive products. What is your opinion of this practice of celebrity endorsement? How do these endorsements affect the way you feel about a celebrity?

The Fame Motive

Online Newspaper Article by
Benedict Carey

Money and power are handy, but millions of ambitious people are after something more.

They want to swivel necks, to walk into a crowded room and feel the conversation stop. They're busy networking, auditioning, talking up their latest project—a screenplay, a memoir, a new reality show—to satisfy a desire so obvious it is all but invisible. Fame.

"To be noticed, to be wanted, to be loved, to walk into a place and have others care about what you're doing, even what you had for lunch that day: that's what people want, in my opinion," said Kaysar Ridha, a recent participant on the reality series *Big Brother*. "It's strange and twisted, because when that attention does come, the irony is you want more privacy."

Until recently, psychologists have ignored fame as a motivator of human behaviour. Now, a small number of psychologists and social scientists have begun to study and think about fame in a different way.

*This article has been edited from it's original form to fit our pages.

Who Wants to Be Famous?

Some people want to be widely known to strangers. Their fame-seeking behaviour seems to come from a desire for social acceptance. In media-rich urban centres, the drive to stand out tends to be oriented toward celebrity, and its hold on people appears similar across diverse cultures. (This is not the same as wanting to have money or power.)

Surveys in Chinese and German cities have found that about 30 percent of adults report regularly daydreaming about being famous. More than 40 percent expect to enjoy some fame at some point in life. Surveys in North America report similar results. Among teenagers, the percentage of people who daydream about fame is higher.

Yet, for all the dreamers, only one or two in 100 (1 or 2 percent) rate fame as their most important goal.

Those who want fame are described by one psychologist as "a distinct type, people who expect to get meaning out of fame, who believe the only way to have their lives make sense is to be famous." Tim Kasser is a psychologist at Knox College in Galesburg, Illinois. "We all need to make meaning out of our lives, and this is one way people attempt to do it." But can fame really bring meaning to your life?

What Are the Odds?

Therapists and researchers have traced the longing for fame to feelings of rejection or neglect. After all, celebrity is the ultimate high-school in-group.

The odds of achieving some measure of fame—a Nobel, an Oscar, a plaque in the Curling Hall of Fame—are so remote that often unrealized ambition changes into grief.

In a 1996 study, two experts (Richard M. Ryan of the University of Rochester and Dr. Kasser, then at Rochester) conducted surveys of 100 adults, asking about their aspirations, guiding principles, and values.

The participants in the study who focused on goals tied to others' approval—like fame—reported much higher levels of distress than those interested in self-acceptance and friendship.

Surveys done since then, in communities around the world, suggest the same thing: aiming for a target that is as elusive as fame, and so dependent on the judgments of others, is treacherous. In other words, searching for fame more often leads to pain and disappointment. It's one thing to want to be a great actor because you love acting. It's another to want to be a great actor because you love having people watch your every move. If you don't become a famous actor, at least you can still do what you love, on a smaller scale.

Is Fame Worth the Trouble?

What about those fame-seekers who actually make it? How do they end up feeling?

Few celebrities confess to wanting to be famous. Even fewer, if any, have agreed to anything like a study of motivation and well-being. So, it's hard to answer that.

Many prominent novelists, actors, writers, and musicians find lasting satisfaction in seeing others moved by their work. And the limos, V.I.P. seating, and private beach parties must help take the edge off the more negative aspects that come with fame.

For all its rewards, fame can be punishing. Scholars, psychologists, and some celebrity biography writers seem to agree on that point.

Public recognition can bring a heightened focus on the self. Mark Schaller, a psychologist at the University of British Columbia, studied the careers of musician Kurt Cobain, jazz musician Cole Porter, and novelist John Cheever.

Dr. Schaller found that all three of these artists began referring to themselves more frequently after they became famous. They were more aware of themselves and of everything they said or did.

And famous people in particular are forced to judge themselves against ideals set by others.

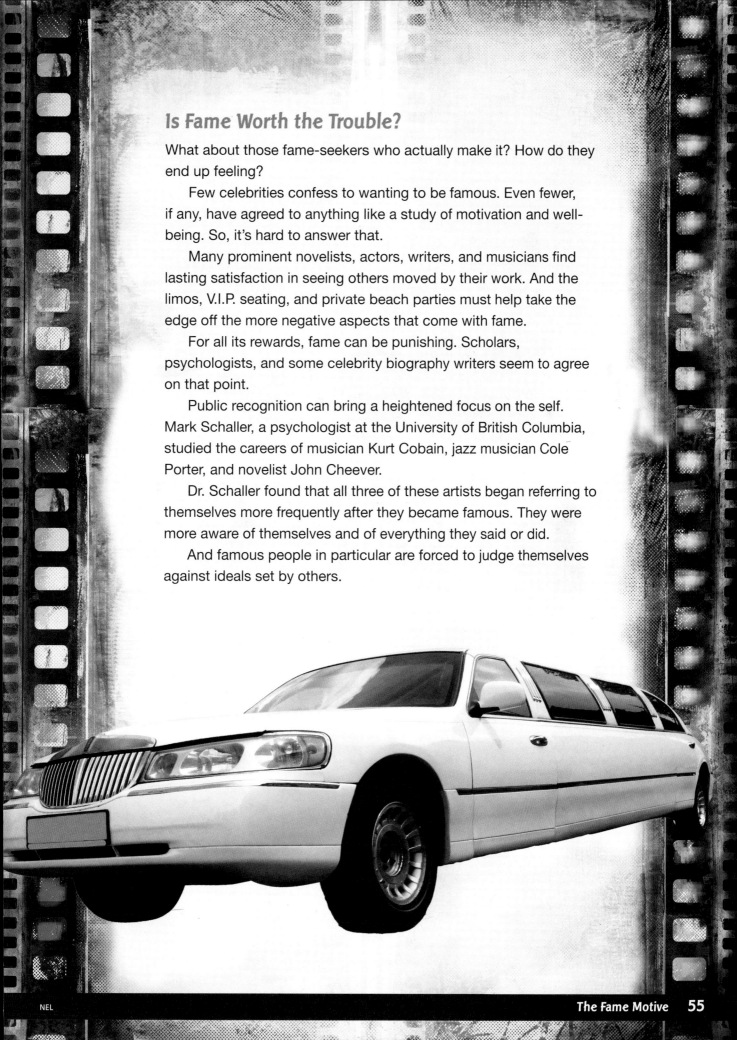

Can We Get Past Fame?

"If you or I hear our own voice on tape, or see ourselves on camera, we might say: 'Wait a minute, I'm a doofus. I'm not the sharp guy I thought I was,' and we can cope with that, we can try harder," Dr. Schaller said.

"But it's a little different if you're a Bruce Willis or somebody. The ideals others have for you are crazy. It's virtually impossible to meet them, and you can't escape this heightened self-awareness."

None of which may stop a single soul from pursuing fame if they're given a chance.

Fame is random, and its effect on any one person is not predictable. Perhaps that is the source of its allure: the unknowns. The secret horrors and joys, the privileges revealed only to those famous few.

In compiling his research, another psychologist, Dr. Brim, thought a lot about how an intense desire to reach fame—this unknowable, alluring state of being—might affect people's behaviour. What happens when fame doesn't happen, but the desire doesn't fade?

"I concluded that several things could happen, and one of them is to find another source of approval," he said. "That might be a great love, if you're lucky. Or perhaps it is a deepening belief in God. But I think many people suffer with the realization that they are not going to be famous. And there's nothing they can do to solve it."

Reflecting

Analyzing Text Patterns: According to this article, why do some people pursue fame? What effect can pursuing fame have on them?

Metacognition: What strategies did you use to help you understand this article? Explain how those strategies helped you.

Critical Literacy: Does this article present a reasonable and believable explanation of the pursuit of fame? What evidence from the article supports your response?

History

The reading strategy you learned in this unit can help you to better understand text in other subject areas. As you read, synthesize the information in this history text.

Selling Canada

Wilfrid Laurier and the Liberal Party formed Canada's government after the 1896 election. Eighteen years of Conservative Party rule were over. The country was ready to begin a new era. Like John A. Macdonald, Wilfrid Laurier believed that large numbers of Western settlers were key to Canada's prosperity. Fortunately for Wilfrid Laurier, conditions in the world and in Canada changed after 1896. These changes made Canada's West more attractive to immigrants than it had been during John A. Macdonald's years.

The task of attracting immigrants was given to Clifford Sifton, who was appointed minister of the interior in 1896. Clifford had clear ideas about the type of immigrants Canada needed and how to encourage them to come to Canada.

A Targeted Audience

In Clifford's view, the best immigrants for Canada were farmers and farm workers. He also had clear ideas about which countries these farmers should come from.

Clifford looked first to the United States for experienced farmers. American farmers would be able to bring some of the goods they would need to start a farm, such as cash, equipment, and animals. He also welcomed people from the United Kingdom. In addition to farming experience, they would bring British loyalty, values, and customs. Finally, he looked for peasants from Central and Eastern Europe because they were used to a climate and geography similar to Canadian conditions. These immigrants would be prepared for some of the challenges of the Canadian prairie.

A Clear Message

Clifford Sifton approached the task of promoting Canada like a salesperson. He had thousands of hectares of farmland to settle, so he launched an advertising campaign. His campaign targeted the immigrants he thought were best for Canada. He used a variety of forms of advertising, but all sent a clear message about the benefits of moving to Canada.

The Canadian government's immigration department spared no expense in promoting the West. Clifford hired more immigration agents and opened immigration offices in Europe and the United States. Immigration offices provided potential immigrants with information about the Prairies and Canada's immigration requirements and procedures.

This Canadian emigration office was located in London, England. It once sponsored an essay-writing contest for British schoolchildren. First prize gave the child's family a free homestead and passage to Canada.

Immigration agents worked with transportation companies to make it easy for immigrants to get to Canada. By 1914, the Canadian Pacific Railway (CPR) was one of the world's biggest ship owners. Many of its ships had third-class sections for people travelling by steerage. Steerage passengers paid the lowest rates. Rates offered by the CPR and other travel companies often included ship passage to Canada and a rail ticket to the West.

The message to immigrants was clear: The Canadian government was ready to assist all suitable farm immigrants. Moreover, getting to Canada was inexpensive and easy.

Immigration agents used a variety of different forms of advertising to sell Canada's West. Their campaigns included posters, pamphlets, pictures, lectures, magazines, slide shows, and travelling road shows. Different techniques were used for specific groups.

Some posters compared Canada to Eldorado. In the sixteenth century, explorers heard stories of a city in the Americas called Eldorado. It was supposed to be filled with gold and treasure.

However, all ads had the same goal: to convince potential immigrants that Canada's West was a land of opportunity.

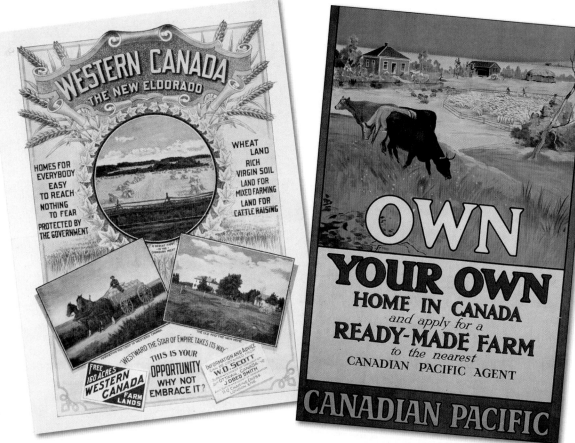

This poster was used to attract American settlers to Western Canada.

The Canadian Pacific Railway actively promoted immigration to Canada's West.

Reflecting

Synthesizing: When you read the title "Selling Canada," what did you think this text might be about? What modern selling techniques did you recall to help you understand these historical methods? How did the historical documents and posters help you better understand this period in Canada's history?

Metacognition: What helped you synthesize as you read this selection? How did synthesizing help you understand and respond to this selection?

Chasing a Dream

How will you make your dreams a reality?

Unit Learning Goals

- evaluate texts while reading
- revise and edit

- communicate effectively
- create public service announcements

- analyze problem/ solution text pattern

Transfer Your Learning: the Arts

How to → # Evaluate Texts

If you tell your friends about something you've read recently, they may ask your opinion of it. When you answer, you are evaluating the text. Strong evaluations are based on questioning the text. You need to **think** about what you already know, **reflect** on what the author is saying, and **decide** whether you agree or disagree.

Questions I Asked of the Text	Answers or Clues in the Text	My Final Opinion or Judgment

Some questions you might ask to evaluate a text:

• Is the information accurate or storyline believable?

• What is the author's message or point of view? Do I agree with it?

• What beliefs does the text seem to express?

• What biases does the text have?

• Does information in the text support, challenge, or add to what I already know?

• What is my response to the text or its viewpoints?

Strong answers to these questions require the following:

• specific details from the text that support your opinion

• specific quotes from the text that show what the author or characters think, feel, or believe

• information you know or believe to be true that supports or contradicts the text

• specific reasons why the author's story or argument is true or lacks credibility

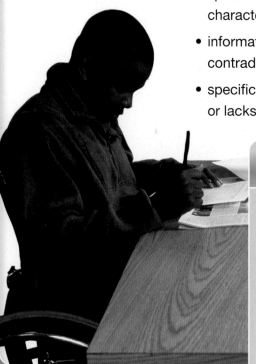

Transfer Your Learning

Across the Strands

Media Literacy: Think about your favourite ad. What evaluative questions could you ask to help you determine whether the ad provides accurate and believable information?

Across the Curriculum

The Arts: When you watch a play or TV show with actors you particularly like, it can be difficult to give a fair evaluation. What questions can you ask to ensure your evaluation is unbiased?

Talk About It
Do you think freedom is important?

Freedom Dreams

Traditional Song with Comic written by Diane Robitaille and illustrated by Ho Che Anderson

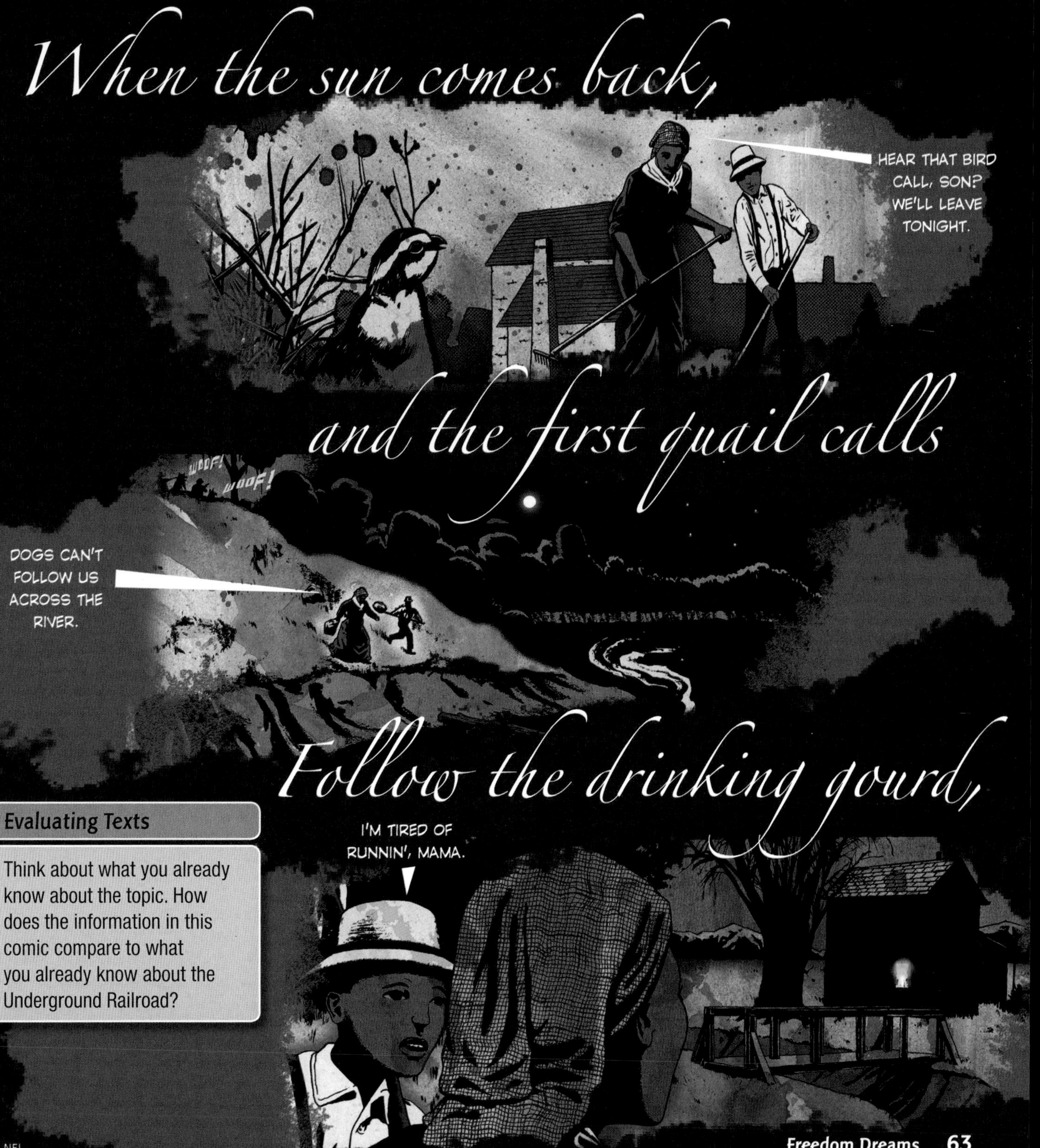

When the sun comes back,

HEAR THAT BIRD CALL, SON? WE'LL LEAVE TONIGHT.

and the first quail calls

WOOF! WOOF!

DOGS CAN'T FOLLOW US ACROSS THE RIVER.

Follow the drinking gourd,

I'M TIRED OF RUNNIN', MAMA.

Evaluating Texts

Think about what you already know about the topic. How does the information in this comic compare to what you already know about the Underground Railroad?

for the old man is waiting

HARRIET'S GONNA LEAD
US TO FREEDOM, SON.

for to carry you to freedom

The hidden messages in the song "Following the Drinking Gourd" helped guide enslaved African-Americans to freedom in the northern United States and Canada. For example, the "old man" in the song is the Mississippi River and the "drinking gourd" is the Big Dipper.

Harriet Tubman was a famous freedom fighter. She made 11 trips to Canada, helping more than 300 Underground Railroad "passengers." They travelled at night, hiding during the day in barns, chimneys, and haystacks.

If you follow the drinking gourd.

The riverbank will make a very good road

Evaluating Texts

Look for clues in the text that tell you what the author believes or values. Think about your own beliefs and values. What do you think the author believes or values? Do you agree or disagree?

TOGETHER, WE CAN BUILD A FUTURE IN THIS COUNTRY.

The dead trees show you the way.

THEY'LL HIRE US TO WASH DISHES.

BUT THEY WON'T LET US ORDER EVEN A SLICE OF TOAST.

Left foot, peg foot, travelling on,

CITY COUNCIL SAYS WE WON'T GET ELECTRICITY OR RUNNING WATER.

BUT THEY'LL PUT A GARBAGE DUMP AT THE EDGE OF OUR TOWN.

Follow the drinking gourd.

The river ends between two hills

RIGHT, BULLDOZERS MOVE INTO AFRICVILLE TO START DEMOLITION IMMEDIATELY.

Follow the drinking gourd.

'COURSE THIS IS MY HOME. MY FAMILY'S LIVED HERE FOR 150 YEARS.

There's another river on the other side,

THE DAY I LEFT MY HOME, A PART OF ME DIED INSIDE.

Evaluating Texts

Look for clues in the text that tell you about the author's bias or point of view. How do you personally respond to this author's message and point of view?

Follow the drinking gourd.

When the great big river meets the little river

Evaluating Texts

Decide whether you agree or disagree with the author's message. Reflect on what the author is saying and how you respond. What message does this text send? How do you respond to it?

Follow the drinking gourd.

Some of the African-Americans who escaped slavery in the United States settled in southern Ontario and Nova Scotia outside of Halifax. Now they fought for freedom from outright racism and for better living conditions.

For example, in Africville in Nova Scotia in the 1960s, the Black community fought to prevent the demolition of their church and homes, and the relocation of their citizens.

In 2002, Africville was declared a national historic site. Today, former residents of Africville still fight for justice and compensation for their descendants.

For the old man is waiting for to carry you to freedom

Reflecting

Evaluating Texts: What line or image in this selection best presents the artist's message or point of view? What is your response to that message?

Metacognition: How did asking evaluative questions help you respond to this selection?

Media Literacy: How does viewing a comic contribute to your understanding of this issue? What other media form (such as a movie, poster, or radio play) could be used to present the same information?

If you follow the drinking gourd.

Talk About It
Many poets write about their dreams. What would you want to say in a poem about your dreams?

Dream Time

Poems by various poets

Hold Fast Your Dreams

From a Poem by Louise Driscoll

Within your heart
Keep one still, secret spot
Where dreams may go,
And sheltered so,
May thrive and grow—
Where doubt and fear are not.
Oh, keep a place apart
Within your heart,
For little dreams to go.

Quintrain

Poem by Sa'id 'Aql, translated by Mansour Ajami

Once … I heard a bird,
an absorbed, ecstatic bird,
eloquently telling
its child:
"Fly away,
soar high:
a few bread crumbs
will suffice you,
But the sky
you need …
the whole sky."

Fantasia

Poem by Eve Merriam

I dream
of giving birth
to
a child
who will ask,
"Mother,
what was war?"

Reflecting

Evaluating Texts: What values or beliefs do all three poets have in common? What evidence in the poems supports your opinion?

Metacognition: What strategies did you use to make sense of and evaluate these poems?

Critical Literacy: Choose one poem. How do you think the poet wants you to respond to that poem? How did you respond?

Talk About It
People who make their dreams come true usually share certain personality traits. What do you think those traits are?

Breaking Free

Online Article by Margaret Jetelina

Her success is no illusion: Chinese-born magician Juliana Chen travels Canada and the globe, amazing audiences with her sleight of hand.

It's hard to take your eyes off Juliana Chen when she is onstage. You watch entranced as she moves, practically floats, in sync with the powerful music that accompanies her. Her face has a hint of a smile. She makes you sit up straight, straining to see her next move and, with a flick of her hand, she makes you gasp.

Juliana is a world-famous magician, and perhaps the best-known female magician today. Her onstage presence is confident, her costumes elaborate, and her star power undeniable. During a phone interview, Juliana speaks softly about days long past as a child performer in China.

"I was a ballerina," she starts. "I trained hard for five years in ballet school. I'd wake up at 5:30 a.m. and get up and warm up. From 9 a.m. to 12 p.m., I'd do ballet, and then I'd get a little break in the afternoon. From 2:30 to 5:30 p.m., I'd attend a different class, sometimes music, sometimes performance, where we learned how to move our eyes, body, hands," she says. After dinner, she then had to attend regular school from 7:30 to 9:30 p.m.

The training was focused and intense. Juliana was actually happy to have been chosen at 12 years of age to join the Hunan Academy for the Performing Arts. She was luckier than most, since the art school was in her hometown, which meant she could visit her family, a luxury that many children didn't have.

At the Hunan Academy, Juliana originally trained as a ballet dancer. Then the Chinese government decided that the circuses needed more talent and Juliana was transferred to the Hunan Acrobatic Troupe. "I had long legs so they trained me to be a foot juggler." But Juliana soon had to give up foot juggling after several acrobatic training accidents severely damaged her legs. While she was recovering, she saw a televised broadcast of the famous Japanese magician Shimada. She couldn't get the performance out of her mind and started paying attention to the magician that she had been working with in the circus.

"I started to develop my own style," she says. "I then had a chance to perform and show my boss." He liked what he saw. Four years later, in 1986, Juliana won first place in China's Best Magician competition.

She became a star magician, but she craved something that China couldn't offer her: a future that she could choose and shape for herself.

Like an escape artist breaking out from a locked box, she found her way to Vancouver, British Columbia. As a performer, she had been given the opportunity to study English in Vancouver, and she took it. "When I flew from Hong Kong to Vancouver, I looked out the window and I felt like a bird. I could fly."

Although she knew she could easily return to her successful magic career in China, Juliana decided to take the leap and immigrate permanently to Canada. It was lonely for her at first. "I was a big star in China, and in Canada no one knew me," she says. "It can be very difficult for newly immigrated people," she says.

As a young Chinese woman who had only known the arts as a profession, she struggled to find where she belonged in Canada, but she stayed brave. "I didn't want to stay in Chinatown. I felt that if you're going to a different country, you have to go out into the country, learn the new language and culture."

Her first job was as a bookkeeper in a furniture store, and she later started her own typesetting and graphics firm. "But being an entertainer was always in my mind. I didn't know what I could do in the future with it here, but I never gave up," she says. Her lucky day came when a reporter for a Chinese newspaper recognized her. "They wrote a full-page story about a Chinese star living in Vancouver."

That article led to her first performance request in Vancouver, at the Chinese Cultural Centre in 1989. "It was a big dinner show, and I realized I didn't have enough stuff to do a full performance. I had brought one of my illusions with me to Canada, but when it went through customs, it got broken."

She stumbled upon a local magic shop and couldn't believe her eyes. "We didn't have shops like that in China. It was the first time in my life I saw one. I was like a big kid, playing with everything there," she says. "The owner was watching me and asked if I was a professional magician." After telling him her story, he invited her to attend a meeting of the Vancouver Magic Circle, and Juliana soon participated in a Vancouver magic competition, where she got a 10-minute standing ovation.

"People started to pay attention to me," Juliana says. She began receiving more awards, accolades, and contracts in North America and around the world, much more than she could have ever achieved in China. In 1997, she won the world title for sleight of hand at the World Congress of Magicians in Dresden, Germany—the first woman and first magician of Chinese heritage to win a world title for a solo act.

Her historic win led to TV specials on NBC and ABC, and a segment on CBC's *The Fifth Estate*. Then came cover stories in magic magazines, interviews in mainstream press, more awards, and more tours.

Today, she happily tours Canada and the world, with regularly scheduled stints in Las Vegas and Germany, but her first home continues to be Canada. "It doesn't matter where I go, I just love coming back to Canada." It was Canada, after all, where the magician was able to break free and discover the tricks to her ultimate success.

Reflecting

Evaluating: What does the author of this selection believe it takes to make your dreams come true? How do you know? How do you respond to that belief?

Metacognition: What question was most useful to you when you were evaluating this text?

Critical Thinking: What detail in this selection do you think is typical of the Canadian immigrant experience?

Talk About It

What are some of the obstacles that prevent people from achieving their dreams?

The Man Who Killed

Oral History retold by Ramona Maher

On Kodiak Island lived a young man. He was a good hunter and trapper on land, and with his dip net and spear he caught many fish. But most of all, the young man wanted to stand in the front of a kayak with a harpoon when the men of the island went out to the deep water for whales and seals.

The young man spent many long hours practising with his harpoon. He would harpoon floating logs, and with each throw the harpoon landed, quivering, in the log.

Eskimo and Beluga. **Silkscreen print by Henry Napartuk (Inuit), Alaska**

the Sea Monster

But when the young man went to the old men of the village to ask whether he could be part of the seal-hunting kayaks, the old men would shake their heads. "No, your father brought bad luck to the village. He harpooned a giant whale, one that was too large for the kayak he was in. The whale pulled the kayak out to sea. Five men of our village were lost."

"I will not be careless," said the young man. "Please let me go." He showed them how he could send his harpoon into a target, straight as a sinew.

The old men still shook their heads. "Yes, you are a good hunter, but you would bring us bad luck out on the sea. Hunt bears here on the island with your bow and arrow. In that way you can be of the most service to your village."

The young man did as the elders told him to do. He killed the giant bears that roamed the island. When he took one of the bears back to his village, there was great feasting.

The young man would not be happy at the feast and the ceremonies. More than anything else, he still wanted to be a harpooner in a kayak.

One day the men set out in their kayaks to go after fur seals. Their kayaks did not get out of the bay. The young man and the women and children of the village stood on the shore, watching the kayaks shoot swiftly through the water, back to the village.

"What is wrong?" called the young man.

The women groaned as they saw in one of the kayaks the lifeless-seeming body of a man.

"A monster," the man was muttering. "A whale with the face of a dog!"

One of the rowers told the young man what had happened. "A great fish, almost like a whale, will not let the boats out of the bay. He lashed with his powerful tail fin and broke up the kayak in which that man was rowing. The harpooner in that boat went under the water, and we never saw him come up again."

A whale with the face of a dog! What could that be? wondered the young man.

The next day, several kayaks ventured out from the village. In less than half an hour the kayaks came nudging back at the shore.

"The whale will not let us get out of the bay," said one of the kayak men. "He means to keep us from harpooning the killer whales or catching the seals."

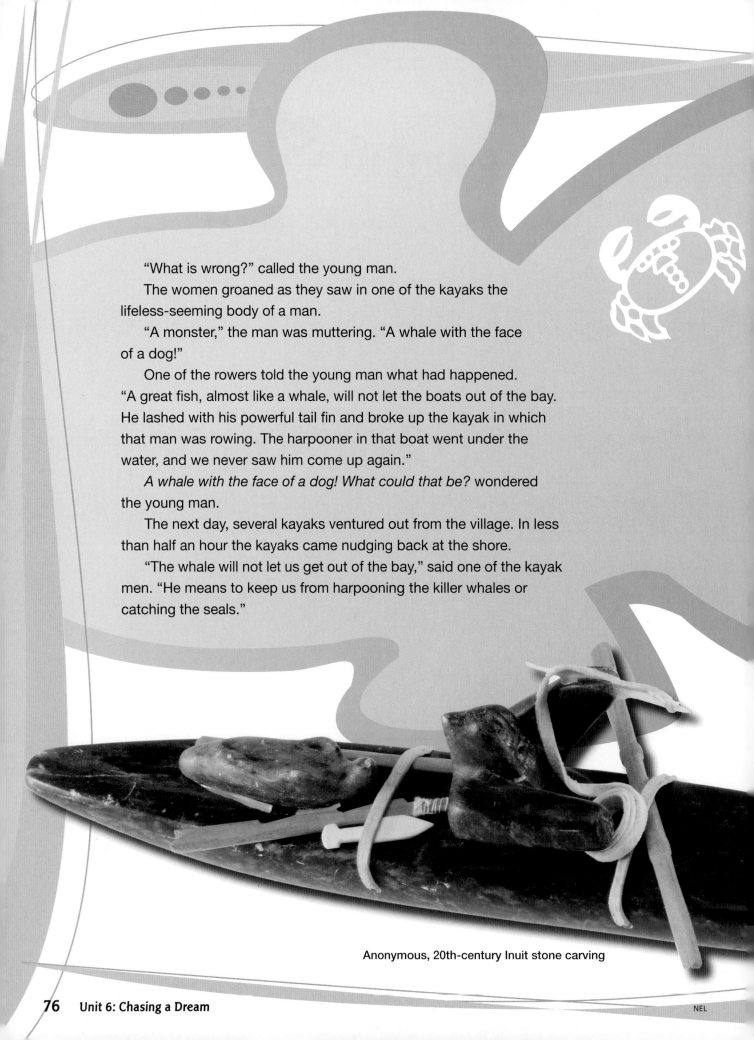

Anonymous, 20th-century Inuit stone carving

Each day one or two kayaks went out into the bay to see if they could slip past the whale with the face of a dog. Each day it was useless. The men just sat around the village, in the sweathouse, talking and trying to think of ways to outwit the monster whale.

No one had any ideas. They were all afraid, thought the young man, *because they remembered the harpooner who had been lost and the rower whose legs had been paralyzed by the great whale's tail fin.*

The young man stood on the highest cliff on the island and looked out to the mouth of the bay. He could see a black object, swimming powerfully around. He saw a spout rise from a blowhole on the creature's back, and he knew it was the monster whale.

"I will come after you, whale," promised the young man. "If I harpoon you, I will be the bravest hunter in the village."

He kept his plan a secret. Dragging his kayak into the trees of the beach, he painted one side of it red. The other side he painted black. With white paint, he painted a crab on the left side of the bow. With yellow paint, he painted a human hand on the right side of the bow. Then he took blue paint and went to the stern of the boat. He painted a blue star on the left side of the stern, and he painted a blue kayak on the right side of the stern.

Then, using a small twig which he broke off a tree as a brush, he painted the same objects on his left hand. He used red paint. He painted a star on his thumb. On the first finger of his left hand he painted a kayak. On the second finger of his left hand he painted a crab, and on his third finger he painted a tiny hand with five fingers.

When the paint had dried, the young man took his harpoon and climbed into the kayak. He sat down on the matting of moss and sticks in the bed of the kayak and began to row. The harpoon lay near him so that he could grasp it quickly.

No one from the village had seen him depart. Out into the bay, farther and farther, the young man rowed. Halfway out, he began to look anxiously for the whale with the face of a dog. It was nowhere in sight.

He kept on rowing. Then the whale rose up beside his kayak, shooting a terrible fountain of water out of its blowhole. The spout was so high it almost hid the sun from sight.

The kayak rocked and almost rolled over, but the young man stood upright and steadied it with his feet. The whale with the face of a dog had made a great circle around the small kayak and was coming toward him, head on. The young man wanted to hide his face from the hideous, red-eyed glare of the great fish.

But he managed to keep his eyes fixed on the whale's eyes. He had the feeling he was safe as long as he kept his gaze fastened directly on the whale.

He began to row slowly back and forth, in front of the whale. First he rowed so that the red side of the kayak faced the monster; then he rowed so that the black side showed.

Anonymous, 20th-century Inuit bone carving

"Do you see that crab, oh whale?"

The whale had a voice like the snarling of a hundred dogs. "I see the crab."

"Do you see the human hand, oh whale?"

"I see the human hand painted on your frail boat," said the whale.

"Do you see the kayak painted on the stern of the boat?" asked the young man.

"Yes," snarled the whale. He made as if to lower his head and charge the kayak.

The young man raised his voice. "Do you see the star painted on the stern of the boat, oh whale?"

A jet of water came from the blowhole of the whale, as if he were laughing. "I smash through stars every night, in the water. I shall smash my way through your star also."

"Wait." The young man held up his hand so that the whale could see the same figures painted on it. At the same time, his right hand tightened around the harpoon.

"The crab means that you are powerless against the power of the sea," said the young man bravely. "You are powerless against the power of man—that is the reason for the human hand painted on the boat. You are weak before the power from above—that is the power of the star which I have brought with me."

The Man Who Killed the Sea Monster

The eyes of the whale with the face of a dog grew redder. "What is the meaning of the kayak sign?"

"The power of man, the power of the sea, and the power from above—all these can seize and kill you," said the young man. "And the kayak has the power to tow you to land."

With a great bellow, the whale headed for the kayak. With great skill, the young man rowed the craft to one side of the whale as it attacked. As the broad back of the fish passed him, he launched his harpoon, into the whale's brain.

Then he held on tightly. The great whale had charged so powerfully that the kayak was being pulled toward shore, towed by the rope of the harpoon which was thrust deep in the whale's body.

The creature crashed on the beach, about a kilometre from the village. The young man crawled out of the kayak and sloshed ashore to view the monster he had captured. It was a great and ugly creature, with the fangs and face of a dog.

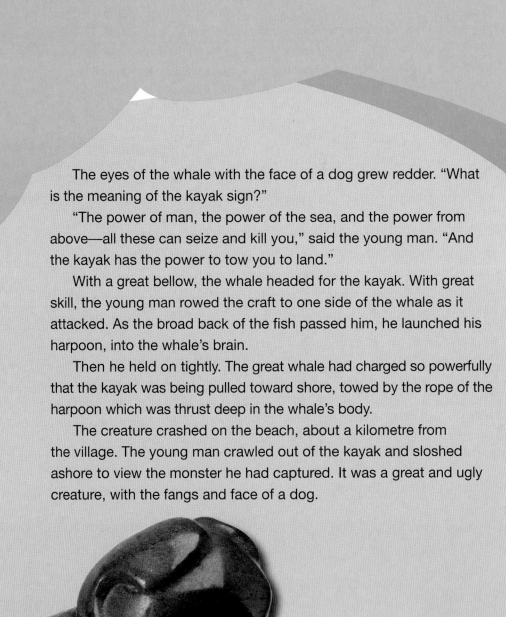

Anonymous, 20th-century
Inuit serpentine stone carving

The villagers had felt the shock of the great whale's body as it slid up on the beach. They streamed down the shore to view the monster.

"This looks like the whale that towed your father's boat out to sea," said an old man, who was so old he knew all the village's history.

One of the most respected sea hunters took the young man's harpoon and put it in his kayak, a sign that he was asking the young man to join his crew.

The young man became one of the best and most honoured hunters on Kodiak Island. Always, when he went out to hunt seals or whales, his boat was decorated with a crab and a hand on the bow, a star and a kayak on the stern.

All this happened a long time ago. But the Kodiak hunters still rely on good luck from the sea and the heavens, and on their skill with the harpoon and kayak. These things bring them home safely with a good catch.

Reflecting

Evaluating Texts: What evaluative questions did you ask as you read this selection? How did you answer those questions?

Metacognition: Evaluating a text includes looking for clues about what the author and/or characters believe or value. What clues in this text helped you figure out what the author and/or characters believe or value?

Media Literacy: Choice of media form may vary with purpose. What media form would you use to tell this story if you were focusing on the hunt? What media form would you use if you were focusing on the hunter achieving his dream?

The Man Who Killed the Sea Monster

How to → # Revise and Edit

Revising and editing are two important steps to take after you've written your first draft.

First, you revise. Reflect on your purpose and your knowledge of the topic and audience, and then use those reflections to revise your text to make it stronger. Making the text stronger may include cutting text, adding text, or changing how the text is organized. Revising can really improve the quality of your writing.

Here are some questions to ask yourself when revising:

- How can I make my *lead* (the opening sentence or paragraph) stronger? For example, you could begin by linking an idea in your text with something your reader already knows.
- Have I organized my writing using the most effective text pattern for my purpose, topic, and audience?
- Did I include information that would be interesting to my readers? Did I include details that will help my readers visualize, or examples that will help them understand?
- Did I avoid including information that I'm confident my readers already know?

Then, you edit your work. Correct any spelling, punctuation, or grammar errors so that your readers will understand your text.

Editing Symbols

Symbol	What It Means
℘	Delete.
∧	Add a word or letter.
=	Capitalize this letter.
/	Make this letter lowercase.
⊙	Add a period.
⩘	Add a comma.
⩗	Add an apostrophe.
#	Put in a space.

Transfer Your Learning

Across the Strands

Reading: How could you use the reading strategy of evaluating to help you as you revise your writing? What evaluative questions should you ask?

Across the Curriculum

The Arts: Preparing a performance (music, dance, or drama) for an audience is a bit like preparing a piece of writing for publication: you have to consider your audience and how best to reach them. Do you agree with this statement? Why or why not?

Talk About It
How do you get ready to compete or perform?

OLYMPIC DREAMS

**Online Diary by Regan Lauscher
from CBC online**

November 9, 2005— Ready or Not!

The dark years are over. We have officially entered into that gleaming and prestigious year all amateur athletes train and live for—Olympic year!

The energy I feel right now is exhilarating. The combination of confidence, excitement, pride, and gratitude pulses through my veins! I am completely motivated—uncontrollably hungry for every single chance to get on the ice, or go to the gym, or improve my equipment.

Maybe it was my medal last year, maybe it's Olympic fever, or maybe it's the four-course Italian cuisine I eat every day that's lifting my spirits, but something down deep inside is telling me that if I have ever had the chance to be great at luge, this is it. Don't get me wrong. It's not telling me that I'll win it all, or that it'll be easy, but it's telling me that it's possible.

Revising and Editing →

Writers begin with a strong lead intended to appeal to their audience. How would you revise this lead to appeal to people who aren't interested in the Olympics?

Revising and Editing →

Making the text stronger may include cutting text, adding text, or changing how the text is organized.

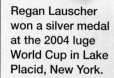

Regan Lauscher won a silver medal at the 2004 luge World Cup in Lake Placid, New York.

I think that moment must come to every athlete. The moment where winning goes from being someone else's reality to your own. When, in the midst of "chasing that Olympic dream," you pick up the pace from a steady jog to a full-out sprint. You graduate from development to developed. You've arrived. Like that monumental Thanksgiving dinner, when you make the move from the plastic-covered kid table to the linen-adorned adult one. When you realize that world champions aren't superheroes. That they're just people who decided to believe that they could win. It's a moment when you decide you can, too.

So here we are in Italy, at the site where in less than 100 days, the world's best amateur athletes will duke it out for that coveted title—Olympic champion.

Last season the luge World Cup here was cancelled because of safety concerns with the newly finished track. Needless to say, I was a little wary this summer when asked about my predictions and goals for the Olympics. What could I say about a track I'd barely slid on? But now, after close to a week of training, I must say that not only are my concerns alleviated and nerves calmer, I am beyond ecstatic to race here!

Maybe it's the fact that I did everything I could in the summer to be as best mentally and physically prepared as I possibly could. Maybe I've just grown as an athlete. And as a person. Maybe it just took me 11 years in this sport to figure things out. Maybe it'll take me even more. But whatever it is, and whatever happens on the ice, I know that I'm ready to do what is in my power to do. And the rest? Well, the rest just doesn't matter.

Revising and Editing

Writers include details that help their readers visualize and understand the text. How does this detail help the reader understand how Regan feels?

Revising and Editing

Good writers organize ideas, information, or events as effectively as possible for their topic, audience, and purpose. How is this text organized? How effectively does the organization reflect the author's purpose?

Reflecting

Reading Like a Writer: What is Regan's purpose in writing this selection? How would the selection be organized differently if her purpose were to explain the demands of her training schedule?

Metacognition: How does your experience as a peer editor help you when it comes to revising or editing your own work?

Critical Thinking: Which of the revision questions on page 82 would be most important if this selection were written with one of Regan's coaches as the sole audience?

I Have Down Syndrome

Know me before you judge me

Magazine Article by Melissa Riggio as told to Rachel Buchholz

When I first started to work on this article, I thought maybe I shouldn't do it. I thought you might see that I have Down syndrome, and that you wouldn't like me. My mom thinks that's silly.

"Have you ever met anyone who didn't like you because you have Down syndrome?" she asks me. She's right, of course. (She usually is!)

When people ask me what Down syndrome is, I tell them it's an extra chromosome. A doctor would tell you the extra chromosome causes an intellectual disability that makes it harder for me to learn things. When my mom first told me I had Down syndrome, I worried that people might think I wasn't as smart as they were, or that I talked or looked different.

I just want to be like everyone else, so sometimes I wish I could give back the extra chromosome. But having Down syndrome is what makes me *me*. And I'm proud of who I am. I'm a hard worker, a good person, and I care about my friends.

A Lot Like You

Even though I have Down syndrome, my life is a lot like yours. I read books and watch TV. I listen to music with my friends. I'm on the swim team and in chorus at school. I think about the future, like who I'll marry. And I get along with my sisters—except when they take my CDs without asking!

Some of my classes are with typical kids, and some are with kids with learning disabilities. I have an aide who helps me take notes and gives me tips on how I should study for tests. It really helps, but I also challenge myself to do well. For instance, my goal was to be in a typical English class by Grade 12. That's exactly what happened this year!

My sisters support me in everything I do, especially in my dream to become a singer.

Dream Job: Singer

I try to think of all the good things in my life. Like that I've published two songs. One of my favourite things to do is write poetry, and this singer my dad knows [Rachel Fuller] recorded some of my poems as singles.

Right now someone else is singing my songs, but someday, *I* want to be the one singing. I know it's going to happen, because I've seen it. One day I looked in the mirror, and I saw someone in my head, a famous person or someone who was *somebody*, and I just knew: I *will* be a singer. It's true that I don't learn some things as fast as other people. But that won't stop me from trying. I just know that if I work really hard and be myself, I can do almost anything.

Horseback riding helps relax me.

See Me

But I still have to remind myself all the time that it really is OK to just be myself. Sometimes all I see—all I think other people see—is the outside of me, not the inside. And I really want people to go in there and see what I'm all about.

Maybe that's why I write poetry—so people can find out who I really am. My poems are all about my feelings: when I hope, when I hurt. I'm not sure where the ideas come from—I just look them up in my head. It's like I have this gut feeling that comes out of me and onto the paper.

I can't change that I have Down syndrome, but one thing I *would* change is how people think of me. I'd tell them: Judge me as a whole person, not just the person you see. Treat me with respect, and accept me for who I am. More important, just be my friend. After all, I would do the same thing for you.

Since this article was published (in National Geographic Kids, *December 2006/January 2007 issue), Melissa had her dream come true. She had the opportunity to sing in public with Rachel Fuller. "Rachel is a good friend…. Without her encouragement and wisdom, my dreams would have stayed just dreams." Sadly, in April 2008 Melissa died of cancer.*

Reflecting

Reading Like a Writer: Melissa begins her article by telling readers that she has Down syndrome and then explaining what it is. Why do you think she begins in this way? If you were revising the article to more strongly emphasize Melissa's music career, what would your lead be?

Metacognition: What do you find challenging when you revise or edit your own writing? How can you overcome that challenge?

Critical Literacy: What does Melissa want us to believe about people with Down syndrome? What evidence in the text supports Melissa's statements?

Talk About It
How long do you expect it to take for your dreams to become a reality?

African Footprint

A Dream and a Vision

**Program Brochure for
Richard Loring's *African Footprint***

Richard Loring's *African Footprint* is an amazing musical and dance performance that gave young South Africans the opportunity to pursue their dreams. The show is described as an "explosive stampede of song and dance that tells the vibrant and diverse history of South Africa."

THE JOURNEY ...

In 1999, Richard Loring, TV and theatre star and show producer, recruited a group of young people from the dusty streets of Soweto*. From hundreds of hopefuls, only 30 young aspiring performers were chosen.

The next year was taken up with vocal classes and intensive dance instruction, which, for most of these youngsters, was their first opportunity to enter the world of professional theatre.

The long hours of rehearsal were rewarded when, on December 31, 1999, *African Footprint* was invited to perform before Nelson Mandela in Block B on Robben Island, the very place where South Africa's leader had been a prisoner for some 18 years.

The result was an explosive and emotional performance televised around the world and seen by over 250 million viewers.

Based on the CNN broadcast, Richard Loring received a deluge of demands that the school start a show, and that show became *African Footprint*, the longest running show in the history of South Africa. It has toured Europe, Australia, China, Israel, and India, and has been invited for command performances twice before Prince Charles and Prince Philip.

Now *African Footprint* is finally embarking on its first North American tour ...

*Soweto is an urban area in the city of Johannesburg, in Gauteng, South Africa. Its name is short for South Western Townships.

MESSAGE FROM CREATOR/DIRECTOR RICHARD LORING

A journey that started with a dream and vision to develop the artistic skills of South African youth through the creation of a unique song and dance experience led me to a World Premiere of the show *African Footprint*.

My resolve, which also became a journey of self-appraisal, was strengthened by a **fortuitous** (lucky) introduction to the fiery words of passion and love of acclaimed poet Don Mattera, and a dynamic exposure to the dramatic **fusion** (blending together) of award-winning choreographers Debbie Rakusin and David Matemela.

No creative process is without pain, frustration, and a lot of soul searching, but each step has truly been a journey of self-discovery, shared with the *African Footprint* company, who have been challenged to extend themselves physically and creatively on a daily basis.

On December 31, 1999, my exposure to the starkness of Block B on Robben Island whilst filming a special Global Broadcast segment with Nelson Mandela, involving the *African Footprint* artists, was truly humbling. This moment became a personal spiritual experience that made the trials and tribulations of my creative journey over four years pale into insignificance.

I am proud to be embarking on our North American tour, which we began in New Orleans, as the first international company to perform since the devastation of hurricane Katrina. May you enjoy each step of our journey through tonight's "Explosive Stampede of Song and Dance."

Richard Loring, Producer

Nelson Mandela, former president of South Africa, was once a political prisoner on Robben Island in Block B. The performance was held in the prison as a tribute to his experience and the experiences of many other political prisoners.

CAST

NORTH AMERICAN TOUR SPRING 2008

Xolani DANGAZELA

Jacobus Johannes GOMES

Mandla HLTATSHWAYO

Shana KOKWANE

Thabo KOMAPI

Tseko LETHOBA

Taryn MAKAAB

Alpheus MALOI

Botho MALOPE

Nokulunga (Lungi) MATHE

Thulani MAVUMA

Mmabatho MOEPWA

Nontle MONDIE

Katlego MOTLHABANE

Tobela MPELA

Themba NDABA

Benevolent (Noel) NDINISA

Jabulani NGCOBO

Gabriel Zakhele NKOSI

Lesago RAMATLHARE

Bongani SIBIYA

Wayne SIYABA

Rachel STOLS

Tebogo TLAHALE

Sandile TWALA

Thulani ZWANE

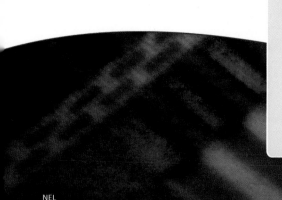

Reflecting

Reading Like a Writer: This selection was written as a program brochure to be given to people as they entered the theatre. If you were able to ask the writer to revise this selection so that it answered your questions, what information would you want included?

Metacognition: A program brochure has a specific purpose and audience. What critical questions should you ask about the information in such a media text?

Media Literacy: Evaluate the design elements in this selection. How does the design influence your response to the selection?

How to ▶ Communicate Effectively

When you have something important to say, you want your audience to listen to you. *How* you share your message makes all the difference in getting your audience to listen. No matter what the occasion, purpose, or audience, the following communication techniques will help your audience follow your presentation:

- Ask questions to involve your audience.

- *Paraphrase* (say in another way) so that your audience hears important information several times.

- Pause or change your speaking pace to highlight important information.

- Use nonverbal techniques for emphasis or to connect with the audience. For example, lean toward the group or make eye contact.

There are also important differences in the communication techniques that you use for different purposes or audiences. Consider these two situations: you have to convince an audience of classmates that people should believe in their dreams; or you have to present to adult judges the results of a science experiment.

Convincing Classmates	Presenting Science Results to Adult Judges
informal structure: appealing to audience interests by beginning with points that will be most convincing to them	*formal structure:* opening statement, main points, conclusion
informal language: vocabulary is persuasive, focused on feelings, may use sensory language	*formal language:* vocabulary is technical and uses scientific terms

Transfer Your Learning

Across the Strands

Writing: You are familiar with various text patterns such as cause and effect, problem/solution, and compare and contrast. How can you use your knowledge of text patterns to help you organize an oral presentation?

Across the Curriculum

Science and Technology: Communicating effectively is important in every subject area. What speaking techniques would you use for a science presentation on cell biology?

Talk About It
Do you think that most adults live their childhood dreams?

MAKING MY DREAMS REALITY

Speech by Dave Cunning

Communicating Effectively

When delivering an oral presentation, you need to consider your purpose and audience. From the title, what do you think Dave's purpose is? As you read, think about the clues that reveal Dave's purpose and audience.

Dave Cunning is an Australian comic book artist who created an organization for publishing local comic book artists. He started an online comic shop—Local Act Comics or LAC—where independent Australian comic book artists can promote and sell their work. After only one year in business, Dave's Local Act Comics was nominated for Production Design of the Year at the Australian Ledger Awards. Here, he speaks to other artists about making his dream come true.

DAVE: Many years ago a good friend of mine asked me, "Dave, what do you want to be when you grow up?"
    After only a few moments I replied, "Al, I want to be a comic book artist."

Communicating Effectively

Good questions can engage and involve the audience. Why is this question a good way to start the speech?

Ten years on and here I am, chasing the dream with Local Act Comics. From the outset, I knew this would be a *hard* road. From the veteran's warnings of lost money to store owners giving the sideways glance with an uninterested, "Australian stuff doesn't sell here …" *(pause)* yet here we are, still pushing on.

It may sound lame but that statement has pushed me in those late, late hours when my hands were too cold to hold a pencil.

I have set a goal for LAC to raise the profile and awareness of the Aussie comics scene, and so far things are looking up. We have a really great group of creators associated with LAC, who are dedicated to pushing the boundaries and making a difference.

Of course, we've had our setbacks. From printers running a month behind to a disheartening lack of enthusiasm when LAC first rolled out asking for contributors to our first anthology, *LAC Presents …*

I think Australian cartoonist Graeme McDonald says it best in his summary of his experience in comics, "navigating my way between those who said they **could** *(pause)* and those that actually **did**."

It's an often unfortunate outcome with Australian comics that everyday life has to come **before** the "hobby." I guess I made the decision along the way that, for me, comics was going to be **part** of everyday life. As with anything in life, the inclusion of one thing often means the exclusion of another, and as far as I'm aware nobody has managed to squeeze any more hours in each day, so we must be content with the fact that only so many words and lines can be scribed in 24 hours, and that we are not super-men and women.

Often, it seems that it is only with the support of those around us *(Dave gestures with spread arms at audience)* that we are able to make a dream such as this one a reality.

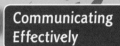 **Communicating Effectively**

Effective speakers pause for emphasis. How does Dave's pause at this point contribute to his message about chasing a dream?

Communicating Effectively

Effective speakers use nonverbal techniques for emphasis or to connect with their audience. Why does Dave spread his arms toward the audience? Why is this a good way to end the speech?

Reflecting

Communicating Effectively: What speaking strategies does Dave use to help his audience understand his message?

Metacognition: What listening strategies do you use to help you understand a speaker? How are those listening strategies connected to the speaking strategies a good speaker uses? (For example, a good listener looks for nonverbal cues.)

Media Literacy: Examine the images that accompany this selection. What can you tell about the artists? How does the text help you interpret the images?

Talk About It
How do you respond when someone asks you what you want to be when you grow up?

Choosing

Monologues by Deborah Karczewski and Diane Robitaille

Setting: family picnic
Characters: Evan, Michelle

EVAN: *(Speaking passionately as if to kind adult relatives.)* I'm going to be a doctor. I've made up my mind. Yes, I *know* I'm only fifteen. Yes, I *know* I have a lotta years to decide. Oh and don't gimme the line about how many years it'll take. I know all about it. Everyone tells me that.

See this scar? *(Gesturing at left leg below hem of shorts.)* Skiing accident. Pretty gross, huh? The bone was sticking right out. Who do you think fixed me up … the Jolly Green Giant? I don't think so.

Lookit this scar, over my eye? *(Pointing to right eye.)* Just one eensy weensy little millimetre lower and Johnny Lo's scissors would've got me good! *(Pausing.)* Right in my eye. And who sewed me together again? NOT the Wizard of Oz!

Look down my throat. *(Opening mouth wide, speaking the next couple of words indistinctly.)* See any tonsils? Nope! Oh, and check out my earlobe! *(Tugging on right ear.)* Almost lost it. Neighbour's dog. I'm a walking disaster. But who can I always count on? Doctors!

(Taking a breath, slowing pace, speaking seriously.) None of those things come even close to what happened to my cousin. Michelle wouldn't even be with us today if doctors hadn't saved her the minute she was born! She couldn't breathe, her heart wasn't beating. She was barely any bigger than my hand—and they operated on her heart!

Talk about amazing! I don't care how long it takes; I'm gonna be a doctor!

MICHELLE: *(Responding quietly to teasing cousins.)* You're right—I'm not that good at baseball. Evan runs faster than me. Lisa hits farther. Ann throws the ball better. *(Pointing to each cousin.)* But you're all older and I'm small for my age.

Gimme a break, though. I've only been playing on a team for two years now. I'm not the best player … but I'm not the worst, either. When I'm not playing, I'm watching baseball. Watching the best players to see what they do. I listen to them talk about how they train and what they eat, too.

(Pausing, then rushing through statement.) Just wait, someday I'm gonna be a great pitcher. Because I know what I want. I want to play baseball professionally. *(Cousins laugh and hoot. Smiling at herself.)*

I know right now there isn't a women's professional team. But there should be. Don't you think that would be fair? Why can't there be a women's professional baseball team? Or women should be allowed to play in the same league as men, don't you think?

Sure, it may be a lot of work and effort to make it happen. Sure, it may never happen. But, you know what Gran always says … you don't know what you can make happen … until you try. Do you 'member that T-shirt she used to wear? "Regret is one long, lonely path." Well, I'm gonna practise and keep trying. Just so I'll never have to think, if only I'd done this. 'Cause I think being disappointed after you've done everything you could think of might be less painful than regretting you didn't even try. What do you think?

Reflecting

Communicating Effectively: What clues help you identify the purpose and audience for these monologues? What is the message of each monologue? How effectively is that message delivered?

Metacognition: What persuasive strategies are used in these oral selections that you could use in your own presentations?

Evaluating: What beliefs or viewpoints are expressed in the text? How do you respond to those beliefs or viewpoints?

How to Create Public Service Announcements

Public Service Announcements (PSAs) are media texts designed to inform people about a specific issue or event. They are usually aired on TV or radio, though they may also appear in print form—in magazines, newspapers, or on billboards. PSAs are unlike typical ads because they are not meant to sell a particular product. Many PSAs focus on public health, safety, or lifestyle issues, for example, exercising regularly.

Check out these frames from a PSA developed by students.

1

Believe YOU Can Achieve

2

NARRATOR: You can choose to stay in school. Give yourself credit by getting all your credits. Options for your future expand when you believe you can achieve your high-school diploma.

3

4

Believe!
Achieve!

5

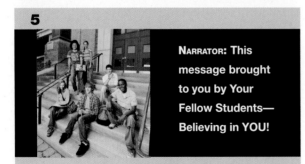

NARRATOR: This message brought to you by Your Fellow Students— Believing in YOU!

6

Meeting weekly, Wednesdays at 3:30 in the cafeteria.

Everyone welcome.

To create a video PSA, you need to present a short, powerful message that tells your audience about a specific cause or issue. Your PSA may suggest possible solutions.

Follow These Steps to Produce a 30-Second Video PSA

1. Select a topic or issue that you feel needs greater public awareness. Research your topic so that you have enough information to create a strong, clear message. Decide what information you will provide and in what sequence.

2. Develop a storyboard.

   a. Think about how many frames you'll need for a 30-second PSA—one for each scene, so between 5 and 10.

   b. Think about what each frame will show. Your storyboard should indicate some of the decisions you're making about actors, props, costumes, setting, and camera angles.

   c. Think about the text or dialogue in each frame. A good PSA uses both text and images to send a strong message and connect with its audience.

3. Rehearse each scene several times so that you are sure of lines, camera use, and pace. Most video PSAs are about 30 seconds long. Time your rehearsal so that you're not too short or too long.

4. Using a digital video camera, film your PSA. Use computer software to put your scenes in the correct order according to the storyboard.

5. Ask others to view your PSA. Based on their feedback, decide how you can make your PSA more effective.

Your PSA should include the following information:

- a description of your cause or issue
- an explanation of why the issue is important
- steps that can be taken to solve or help with the issue
- who you are
- how others can contact your organization

Select camera angles that enhance your message. For example, a *wide shot* reveals your setting. *Close-ups* can give your speaker sincerity and credibility.

Transfer Your Learning

Across the Strands

Oral Communication: What have you learned so far in this unit about communicating effectively that might help you create a more effective PSA?

Across the Curriculum

Health: If you were asked to create a PSA in health class, what health issue would you choose? Who would be your target audience?

UNDERSTANDING
MEDIA
STRATEGIES

▶ Creating
Public Service
Announcements

Talk About It
What catches your attention when you view a PSA?

YOUR HEAD VS CONCRETE

Public Service Announcement from ThinkFirst Canada

Do you dream of ollies, crooked grinds, or hardflips? In your dreams, are you wearing a helmet? ThinkFirst Foundation of Canada has a mission to "prevent brain and spinal cord injury through education aimed at healthy behaviours in children and youth." Check out their PSA on helmet safety.

Creating Public Service Announcements

A PSA informs people about a specific issue using a short, powerful message. What do you think the message of this PSA will be?

Creating Public Service Announcements

A good PSA uses text and images to send a strong message and connect with its audience. How does this PSA connect strongly with its target audience?

Opening Scene: Young teenager on skateboard slides to stop at top of concrete structure. Setting is a skateboard park with ramps and rails. Sound effects throughout: skateboard wheels across concrete.

SKATEBOARDER: I'll start with an ollie.
Camera follows skateboarder through moves as described. Camera angles shift—from above skateboarder to below.

SKATEBOARDER: Go to a frontside melon. Into a crooked grind on the rail.
Skateboarder jumps from ramp to rail to ramp. Moving quickly, quick shots cut from head to feet to skateboard to hands to ground to sky. Cropped shots of feet, board, or hand convey intensity of movements.

SKATEBOARDER: Into a frontside 180. Set up for a frontside 3, 3 flip.
Skateboarder slides down rail. Tight shot on skateboarder's board and legs as he crouches for next move.

SKATEBOARDER:
Back side board slide.
Sets up to hardflip …
Rapid movement of camera as it spins to follow action. Skateboarder's hand appears, hitting concrete ramp.

SKATEBOARDER: … then … ugh!
Closing scene, riderless skateboard slides across concrete, rolls up slight incline, then down. Sound effects: wheels on concrete, then distant shush of traffic.

Text on screen and logo appear: YOUR HEAD vs CONCRETE and THINK FIRST— WEAR A HELMET

think first
WEAR A HELMET

← **Creating Public Service Announcements**

A good PSA delivers the message that the issue is important or serious. How is the seriousness of this issue conveyed?

← **Creating Public Service Announcements**

A good PSA usually includes information about the organization and how it can be reached. What organization created this PSA? Why do you think this organization hasn't included information about how to contact it?

Reflecting

Creating PSAs: A good PSA usually gives you a detailed description of the issue and explicit steps to resolve it. This PSA spends 25 s on entertaining skateboarding scenes and 3 s on its critical message: wear a helmet. Why do you think this PSA does that? Would you judge this PSA as effective? Why or why not?

Metacognition: What's more likely to catch your attention when you view a PSA, the images or the words? What does that tell you about the way you learn?

Critical Literacy: An organization that is advocating the wearing of helmets used an actor who did not wear a helmet during most of the filming. How does that knowledge affect your response to the PSA?

APPLYING
MEDIA
STRATEGIES

▶ Creating
Public Service
Announcements

Talk About It

What choices do you make every day that help you realize your dreams?

CHOOSE

**Public Service Announcement
from Concerned Children's Advertisers**

Opening Scene: Close-up on young girl, camera moving across her face as she says the word You. To face of boy also saying You. Rapid cuts lead from one youth to another, to a group of youths to another. Some are standing or sitting still—facing the camera, others are running across the screen or away from the camera. Each is saying one or more words of the script. At the same time, voice-over repeats the same text. Some speakers overlap. Voices whisper, shout, and speak normally.

You.

You can choose.

You can choose to be alone.

You can choose to be a friend.

You can choose.

Choose.

You can choose from seventy shades of blue.

You can choose to ignore.

You can choose to run wild.

You can choose not to watch.

You can choose to keep a secret.

To be shy.

You can choose to believe that—

—that dogs understand us.

You can choose to be bored.

You can choose to dream.

I.

You.

Choose …

'Cause you can.

Closing shot: Text on screen: Logo for Concerned Children's Advertisers. Health Canada/Santé Canada logo.

Reflecting

Creating PSAs: What do you think is the most important information to include when creating a PSA?

Metacognition: What have you learned from viewing other PSAs that will help you create your own? What have you learned from examining this PSA that will help you analyze others?

Evaluating: What do the producers of this PSA believe or value? How do you respond to those beliefs or values?

Problem/Solution

Problem/solution text pattern describes one *or more* problems and then suggests one *or more* possible solutions. Sometimes the solutions are independent of each other; sometimes one solution builds on the last.

For example, say you wrote an advice columnist about the following problem: You want to volunteer in a way that interests you—rescuing animals, saving the environment, helping at the local senior centre—but you only have time for one of these and can't decide.

The advice columnist might suggest the following solutions:
Ask people who are already volunteering in each area what they like about their work. *OR* Try out each for a week and then come to a decision. *OR* Think of a way to combine two or more of your interests—perhaps taking a dog to visit people in the senior centre.

Problem/solution text pattern sometimes follows this structure.

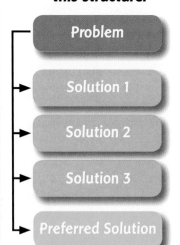

Writers sometimes explain which solution they prefer. Whether they explain or not, as an active reader, think about which solution is best and how that solution can be put into action. Ask yourself: Is this the most practical solution? What are its benefits? Drawbacks?

Problem/solution text pattern is used in informational texts such as advice columns, magazine and newspaper articles, and political speeches. The use of headings may help you identify the problem or solutions. Key words connected with this pattern are *problem, solution, solved, resolved, the evidence shows, propose, conclude.*

Transfer Your Learning

Across the Strands

Oral Communication: Oral presentations sometimes try to inform an audience about how to solve a problem. How would you use problem/solution text pattern to organize an oral presentation effectively?

Across the Curriculum

Science and Technology: Problem/solution text pattern is very common in science writing. If you were developing an essay about the problem of melting polar ice caps, what possible solutions would you include?

Talk About It

Why do so many people dream of being movie stars?

DREAMING OF STARDOM

Profile by Tanya Lloyd Kyi

Stardom ... it's not easy breaking into show biz. Every year, tens of thousands of *aspiring* (rhymes with *perspiring* but means "hopeful" or "ambitious") actors audition for the big role, the one that will get them an Oscar, win them a Cannes Film Festival Award, or earn them a million bucks and a lasting place in the minds and hearts of viewers. Very few succeed. So, how do you become famous? Well, some people might say, "Where there's a will, there's a way." Others would say, "You have to hope for a lucky break." What follows is the story of how one unknown comic made his dream of stardom a reality.

**Problem/Solution
Text Pattern**

Problem/solution text pattern clearly identifies the problems. From this heading, what do you predict will be the main problem Jim Carrey faces?

→ ## Comic Rejection!

Fourteen-year-old Jim Carrey could hear the blood beating in his ears as he walked onto the stage at Yuk Yuk's Komedy Kabaret in Toronto. The city's first comedy club was actually just a local community centre, transformed with spotlights, a backdrop, and a swirl of small tables. Each week, one paid professional comic would perform, along with five to ten amateurs.

In 1976, one of those amateurs was Jim. He was used to performing for friends and family, but standing on stage felt incredibly different. When he tried a few impressions of famous people and didn't get many laughs from the crowd, he began to panic. With good reason—Yuk Yuk's had a cruel way of getting rid of uninspiring comics. After a few minutes, one of the managers reached over with a large hook, snagged it on Jim's waist, and pulled him offstage. Meanwhile, above the recorded sounds of a car crash, the announcer said, "Yes! It's another Yuk Yuk's disaster!"

School and Family Problems

For many aspiring comics, that kind of rejection at 14 would have put an end to all thoughts of a career. But as the youngest of four children, Jim had grown up knowing that silliness and crazy jokes were a sure way to gain attention. He'd already perfected his role as the class clown at school.

Problem/Solution Text Pattern →

The use of headings may help you identify the problem(s) or solution(s). What problems are identified with this heading? What solution is suggested in the heading on page 107?

Some Popular Jim Carrey Films

Horton Hears a Who! (2008)
Fun with Dick and Jane (2005)
Lemony Snicket's A Series of Unfortunate Events (2004)
Over the Hedge (2004)
Bruce Almighty (2003)

The Majestic (2001)
How the Grinch Stole Christmas (2000)
Simon Birch (1998)
The Truman Show (1998)
Liar, Liar (1997)

One of Jim's elementary-school report cards read: "Jim finishes his work first and then disrupts the class." But not all of his teachers discouraged him. One was so impressed by his imitations that she invited him to perform at the Christmas assembly. Another promised that if he worked well all day, he could put on a routine for the class every afternoon, an opportunity that Jim loved.

Maybe Jim needed to keep making jokes because life at home was so difficult. After several years of working together at a local factory under nightmarish conditions, the family quit and spent eight months living out of a camper van. Jim quit school at 16 and got a job at a picture frame factory, but his constant joking cut into his production, and he was fired after six months.

If At First You Don't Succeed …

Jim was convinced there was something better than factory work in store for him. With his father's encouragement, Jim made an appearance on a local telethon and performed a comedy act at a Scarborough restaurant. Then, with this experience in front of strangers to call on, he went back for a second try at Yuk Yuk's Komedy Kabaret.

 Problem/Solution Text Pattern

A single problem can have one or more solutions. How was Jim's willingness to go back for a second try a solution to his initial problem?

The Cable Guy (1996)
Ace Ventura: When Nature Calls (1995)
Batman Forever (1995)
Dumb and Dumber (1994)
The Mask (1994)
Ace Ventura: Pet Detective (1994)

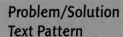

Problem/Solution Text Pattern

Solutions to a problem may be independent of one another, or one solution may build on the last. How did Jim Carrey build on solutions to his initial problem?

→ Armed with several more years of practice, Jim managed to overcome his stage fright and crack up the audience with his impressions and contortions. Within just a few months, he'd moved from the amateur spot to paid performances. And at the age of 17, he decided to go for the big time—he moved to Los Angeles and began performing at a popular club there.

It didn't take long for his big break to arrive. Rodney Dangerfield was in the audience one night and was so impressed by Jim's act that he invited the teen to open for him during his next tour.

... Try, Try Again

Jim was on his way to comedy fame. In 1981, he appeared in his first film. Then, in 1994, he earned international attention with his role in *Ace Ventura: Pet Detective.* He went on to appear in *The Mask, Dumb and Dumber, Batman Forever, Liar Liar,* and *Fun with Dick and Jane.* He also expanded his acting résumé to include more serious roles.

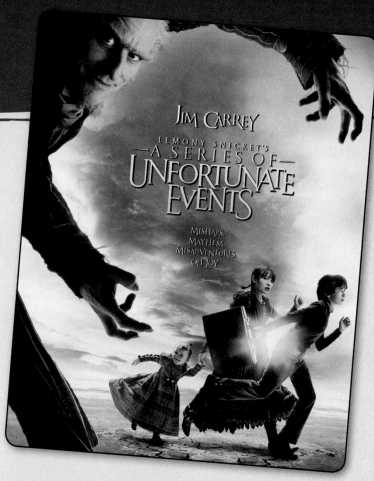

Now, Jim is one of the highest-paid comedic actors in Hollywood; Jim has certainly achieved his childhood dreams. As well, as he gained success and fame as a comedian, Jim resolved his childhood problems of poverty and difficult living conditions.

 Problem/Solution Text Pattern

Key words can signal problem/solution text pattern. What key words in this selection help you identify the pattern?

Reflecting

Analyzing Text Patterns: In your opinion, how clearly does this article state the problem(s) and solution(s)? What evidence in the text supports your answer?

Metacognition: How does analyzing the text pattern affect your response to the text?

Critical Literacy: What viewpoint does the author of this selection hold? Given that viewpoint, what questions should you ask of this selection?

Talk About It
Why is being stubborn sometimes a good thing?

Dancing
toward a
Dream

Evelyn Hart: A Dancer's Progress
Profile by Tanya Lloyd Kyi

*Most famous dancers started when they
were young children of three or four. They
spent years in intensive training. Like aspiring
actors, dancers who want to be famous
have to work hard, get lucky, and have that
special something that puts them above
all the others who want the same thing. It's
a hard life and only a few succeed. Some
dancers face many setbacks before they
succeed; most never get the chance to show
that they too have what it takes. What
follows is the story of one Canadian dancer
who overcame the problems in her path and
became a world-renowned ballerina.*

Early Dreams, Early Reality

When Evelyn stepped into the National Ballet School in 1967, she was 11 years old. She had never taken a dance lesson. She didn't even own a leotard. But when she heard that the prestigious ballet school was holding auditions, she begged her parents for the chance to attend. Ever since she had seen her first ballet on TV, she had dreamed of becoming a dancer.

Evelyn eyed the other girls nervously. Every one of them had a proper leotard and slippers. And as instructors led them through the audition, it was obvious that everyone else had taken lessons before. None of the instructors paid attention to Evelyn, struggling with new steps and positions. She had studied ballet books for *months*, but it wasn't enough.

When the letter from the National Ballet School arrived at her Ontario home, it said that Evelyn didn't have a dancer's body. She was *crushed*. But not for long! She pestered her mother for lessons, and two years later, this time with more confidence and experience, she auditioned again. Again, she was rejected.

Determined or Just Plain Stubborn?

Evelyn was not easily discouraged. In 1970, after her family moved to a town near London, Ontario, she began training with Dorothy and Victoria Carter. She convinced her father to install a barre in her bedroom and she spent *hours* stretching and practising. She completed *two* years of lessons in a *single* year, and in 1971, when she was 15, she auditioned a *third* time for the National Ballet School.

This time, she was accepted—with a full scholarship! But she soon faced a new problem. The *intense* pressure Evelyn placed on herself and the demands of the school proved too much. Because of that stress, by December Evelyn's weight had dropped to 34 kg. She was forced to leave the school and return home. The following fall, she found her place had been given to someone else.

A counsellor encouraged Evelyn to develop other interests, to give up the idea of becoming a dancer. An easy solution that many others might have taken. But Evelyn wasn't ready to give up.

Seeking a Place to Dance

In 1972, Evelyn travelled to New York for summer workshops. There, she won the attention of her instructors and an invitation to train in New York once she finished high school. Finally, Evelyn's confidence grew.

In 1973, at age 17, she auditioned for the Royal Winnipeg Ballet's school, where instructors dubbed her "the wild one." They accepted her immediately. Within three years, she finished her training and entered the Royal Winnipeg Ballet. Soon she was dancing major roles in such ballets as the *Nutcracker* and *Sleeping Beauty*. By 1979, she was a principal dancer.

Evelyn receives the Order of ▶
Canada from Adrienne Clarkson.

But Evelyn's crowning achievements came in 1980. First, she won a bronze medal at the World Ballet Concours in Japan. Then, she travelled to Varna, Bulgaria, to compete in the dance world's most famous arena—the Varna International Ballet Competition. For 16 days, she danced in front of countless judges and audiences. It was soon clear that the audiences loved her. But would the judges?

Achievement and Glory

They did! She won the gold medal and, even more exciting, an Exceptional Artistic Achievement Award. Within days, newspapers were calling Evelyn the best young dancer in the world. Invitations poured in from around the world. Could Evelyn dance in Paris? In New Orleans?

Today, Evelyn has toured North America, Europe, and Asia. The Canadian government has awarded her the Order of Canada. The young girl who dreamed of becoming a professional dancer is a resident guest artist with the Royal Winnipeg Ballet. Evelyn faced her early difficulties and problems squarely. With determination and a refusal to give up, she made her dream a reality.

Evelyn is honoured with a star on
the Canadian Walk of Fame. ▶

Reflecting

Analyzing Text Patterns: What helps you identify this selection's problem/solution text pattern?

Metacognition: How does identifying the text pattern help you understand and respond to the selection?

Critical Literacy: How would the emphasis or perspective of this story be different if it were told in the first person?

Dancing toward a Dream

The Arts

The reading strategy you learned in this unit can help you to better understand text in other subject areas. As you read, ask yourself questions to evaluate these images and the text.

Stream of Dreams

Fact Sheet from Stream of Dreams Murals Society

What is Stream of Dreams™?

- Stream of Dreams is an eco-education program with a focus on water, watersheds, streams, and oceans, which creates a lasting community art legacy to beautify and inspire the whole community.

- A British Columbia non-profit and registered Canadian charity, the Stream of Dreams Murals Society's mission is to educate communities about their watersheds, rivers, and streams while dazzling them with the charm of community art.

The program, which has been presented at more than 200 schools and community events in three provinces to more than 68 000 participants since its inception in 2000, asks and answers the following questions:

- Where is your local stream? Where does the water come from? Where does it go?

- How do storm drains work? Where do house drains go? How are you connected to fish habitats?

- Where does your drinking water come from?

- What changes can we all make in our daily lives to protect and conserve water for fish and people?

- How can we all help others, especially the adults, learn the answers to these questions?

After discussing these questions, each participant paints a wooden fish to help create a lasting community art legacy, a fence mural made up of hundreds of "Dreamfish" reminding everyone to take care of our local waterways.

How, when, and where did Stream of Dreams get started?

The Stream of Dreams program grew out of the tragedy of the 1998 poisoning of all aquatic life, including 5000 fish, in Byrne Creek in Burnaby, B.C., through the storm drain system. The project was conceived by Louise Towell and Joan Carne, Byrne Creek watershed residents, as a positive, hopeful, and beautiful way to raise awareness of the local creek, beautify the neighbourhood, and build community pride. Byrne Creek Streamkeepers, many community members, and the seven elementary schools in Byrne Creek watershed created the first project at Edmonds and Kingsway in Burnaby for B.C. Rivers Day 2000.

And after eight years?

The Stream of Dreams Murals Society has trained and licensed ten teams across B.C., Ontario, and Alberta to use its trademarked and copyrighted program and has presented the program in Washington state. Demand for the program continues to grow, as people want to learn more about how they can protect the environment while beautifying their community. This little born-in-B.C. project is really growing!

What is Stream of Dreams accomplishing?

- Connecting participants and passers-by across Canada to their environment, watershed, and community.

- Expressing hope for the future and reminding people of their role in making positive change for the environment and their community.

- Inspiring behavioural change to protect water and aquatic habitat.

- Building bridges between different community groups.

- Allowing participants to explore their creative side.

- Beautifying in a joyful way.

- Allowing people to be advocates in a gentle but persuasive way.

- Stimulating discussion while inspiring stewardship.

- Identifying neighbourhoods that are becoming watershed wise.

- Influencing municipal governments—planning, engineering, and parks, recreation, and culture departments.

- Engaging whole communities to think about the water that moves through their lives through a highly interactive and imaginative project.

- Giving children hope and showing them the power of a dream.

Reflecting

Evaluating: The creators of this selection value *eco-literacy* (the ability to understand natural systems that make life on earth possible). What evidence in the text reveals that this is something they value? How do you respond to those values?

Metacognition: What questions did you ask yourself to help you evaluate the selection? What other strategies helped you evaluate the text?

Selections Grouped by Theme and Form

Index

Credits

Text

3–5 "How To Be Cool" from *Never Hit a Jellyfish With A Spade* by Guy Browning. © 2004, 2005 by Guy Browning. All rights reserved. Reprinted with permission of the author. 6–11 "Advertising in Disguise" from *Made You Look: How Advertising Works and Why You Should Know* by Shari Graydon © 2003, Annick Press Ltd. 12–17 Reprinted with permission from CBC.ca. 18–21 1958, King Publications. By permission of the author's estate and the Sternig & Byrne Literary Agency. 26–27 Reprinted with permission from Mary Taylor. 28–31 Printed with permission of the author. 33–35 "Practically Twins" from ACTING NATURAL by Peg Kehret © 1991 Meriwether Publishing Ltd. www.meriwether.com. Used by permission. 36–37 Alan Cross, Host, "The Ongoing History of New Music." Printed with permission. 44 Agency: Trigger Communications and Design, Ltd. Advertiser: Calgary Zoological Society. Printed with permission. 47–51 Courtesy of ABC NEWS.com. 52–56 From *The New York Times*, 8/22/2006 © 2006 The New York Times. All rights reserved. Used by permission and protected by the Copyright Laws of the United States. The printing, copying, redistribution, or retransmission of the Material without express written permission is prohibited. 57 © JIM TOOMEY, KING FEATURES SYNDICATE. 58–60 From *Their Stories, Our History* © 2007 Nelson Education Ltd. Reproduced by permission. www.cengage.com/permissions. 68 From *Hold Fast to Your Dreams*, a poem by Louise Driscoll. Appeared first in the New York Times of 1918. 69 "Quintrain" By permission of Dr. Mansour Ajami, translator; "Fantasia" From A SKY FULL OF POEMS by Eve Merriam. Copyright © 1964, 1970, 1973, 1986 by Eve Merriam. Used by permission of Marian Reiner. 70–73 Margaret Jetelina is editor of the Canadian Immigrant magazine. Reprinted with permission. 74–81 "The Man Who Killed the Sea Monster" by Ramona Mayer. Reprinted with the permission of the Estate of Ramona Mayer. 83–84 By Regan Lausher, CBC.CA. Reprinted with permission. 85–87 National Geographic Magazine. Reprinted with permission. 88–91 Starvox Entertainment Inc. Reprinted with permission. 93–95 Dave Cunning, Director, Local Act Comics Pty, Ltd. Reprinted with permission. 96 "Part of the Miracle" from TEENS HAVE FEELINGS, TOO! By Deborah Karczowski © Copyright 2000. Meriwether Publishing Ltd. Used by permission. www.meriwether. com. 100–101 © Think First Canada. Reprinted with permission. 102–103 © Concerned Children's Advertisers. 105–109 From *Canadian Boys Who Rocked the World* by Tanya Lloyd, pp. 92–93 Whitecap Books. Reprinted with permission. 110–113 From *Canadian Girls Who Rocked the World* by Tanya Lloyd Kyi, pp. 28–31. Whitecap Books. Reprinted with permission. 114–116 Photos and text courtesy of Stream of Dreams Murals Society.

Photos

Cover (young man with guitar) paulaphoto/Shutterstock; (musical background) argus/Shutterstock; (theatre lights) Vladislav Bukin/Shutterstock; (crowd) dwphotos/Shutterstock; (goldfish-shark) Tim Hawley/Getty Images; (shark fin) iStockphoto.com/Jim Lopes. 1 (seahorse) kristian sekulic/Shutterstock; (horse) tereh/Big Stock Photo; (background) Elisei Shafer/Shutterstock. 2 © Mary Kate Denny/PhotoEdit. 3–5 (background) Noah Strycker/Shutterstock; 3 & 5. 5 AZ/Shutterstock. 6–11 (background) © iStockphoto.com/Bill Noll. 6 Kareem Black/Shutterstock. 7 Oliver Rossi/Getty Images. 8 © Steven Vidler/Eurasia Press/CORBIS. 9 Getty Images. 10 Yurlov Andrey Aleksandrovich/Shutterstock. 11 Jerry Horbert/Shutterstock. 12 andresr/Shutterstock. 13 Patricia De La Rosa/Getty Images. 14 Time & Life Pictures/Getty Images. 15 © Markku Lahdesmaki/CORBIS. 16 Gordon Gahan/National Geographic Stock. 17 Photo by Jacques Henri Lartigue © Ministère de la Culture France/AAJHL. 18–21 (bricks) Fernando Jose Vasconcelos/Shutterstock; (bars) Stephen Aaron Rees/Shutterstock. 18 Photodisc/Getty Images. 18–19 Photodisc/Getty Images. 19 Photodisc/Getty Images. 20 (Asian woman) rubberball/Getty Images; (girl with pony tails) Photodisc/Getty Images; (girl smiling) Photodisc/Getty Images. 21 Photodisc/Getty Images. 22 © Bill Aron/PhotoEdit. 23–25 Ozger Aybike Sarikaya/

Shutterstock. 26–27 Petrov Stanislav Eduardovich/Shutterstock. 28–31 nix/Shutterstock. 28 Image courtesy of Taqralik Partridge. 32 Michael Newman/PhotoEdit. 33–35 Juan Facundo Mora Soria. 38 Courtesy President's Choice ®. 39 Courtesy of www.gethipgetgreen.com (8666–782–7259). 40–43 Larisa Lofitskaya/Shutterstock. 40–41 Courtesy College Ontario/Smith Roberts Creative Communications. 42 Courtesy Saatchi & Saatchi. 43 (Cloverfield) PARAMOUNT PICTURES/THE KOBAL COLLECTION; (Narnia) WALT DISNEY PICTURES/WALDEN MEDIA/THE KOBAL COLLECTION. 44–45 (background composite) emin kuliyev/Shutterstock; Michael O. Brown/ Shutterstock; Terry Chan/Shutterstock. 46 © iStockphoto.com/Jacob Wackerhausen. 47–51 © Pitris/ Dreamstime.com. 47 Getty Images. 48 (both) Getty Images. 49 Getty Images. 50 Peter Kramer/ Getty Images; Nick Laham/Getty Images. 51 NBAE/Getty Images. 52–57 (film strips) Gordan/ Shutterstock. 52 emin kuliyev/Shutterstock. 53 Losevsky Pavel/Shutterstock. 54 egd/Shutterstock. 55 Boguslawa Jamka/Shutterstock. 56 (statue) Chepe Nicoli/Shutterstock; (trophy) Mike Tolstoy/ photobank.kiev.ua/Shutterstock. 58 LAC C–126299. 59 LAC C–063257. 60 (Own Your Own Home) GA Poster–21; (Western Canada) LAC C–085854. 61 Jason Stitt/Shutterstock; (background) Noel Powell, Schaumburg/Shutterstock. 62 © Myrleen Ferguson Cate/Photo Edit. 68–69 (background) © iStockphoto.com/Duncan Walker. 68 © iStockphoto.com/Daniel Cardiff. 69 (birds) © iStockphoto. com/Alejandro Raymond; (teens) © iStockphoto.com/Izabela Habur. 71 left: Photo by Zakary Bellamy; 71 right, 72–73 © Juliana Chen.74 Mingei International Museum / Art Resource, NY. 76–77 McCord Museum ME988.138.49–P1. 79 McCord Museum M999.105.21–P1. 80 McCord Museum ME987.98.7–P2. 82 Laurence Gough/Shutterstock. 83 The Canadian Press (Adrian Wyld); 85–87 (background) argus/Shutterstock. 85 (microphone) MaxlX/Shutterstock; 85–87 (piano) evan66/Shutterstock. 85–87 Photos of Melissa Riggio: Annie Griffiths Belt/National Geographic Stock. 88–91 (background) Stephen Lynch/Shutterstock; all other photos: Courtesy Starvox Entertainment Inc. 92 © Michael Newman/Photo Edit. 93–95 (background) Ozerina ann/ Shutterstock; atanasis/Shutterstock; (illustrations and logo) Courtesy Dave Cunning, Director, Local Act Comics. 96–97 Barrie Rokeach/Getty Images. 98 (three boys) Tad Denson; (kids on steps) Digital Vision/Getty Images; (hallway) Ken Hurst/Shutterstock. 100–101 Screenshots courtesy Think First Canada; (background colour) ella_E/Shutterstock; (skateboarder) George Unger IV/Shutterstock. 102–103 All screenshots © Concerned Children's Advertisers. 102–103 (background) nagib/Shutterstock; © iStockphoto.com/mecaleha. 102 (boy pointing) Miroslav Tolimir/Shutterstock. 103 (girl jumping) © Jupiter Photos, 2008. 105–109 (background, hibiscus) sunnyfrog/Shutterstock. 108 PARAMOUNT/THE KOBAL COLLECTION. 109 MORGAN CREEK INTERNATIONAL/THE KOBAL COLLECTION. 110 (ballet shoes) Filipchuck Oleg Vladimirovich/Shutterstock. 111 Sarah Nicholl/Shutterstock 112 (ballet shoes) Sean Nel/ Shutterstock; (Eveyln Hart) The Canadian Press/Winnipeg Free Press (Ken Gigliotti). 113 (walk of fame) The Canadian Press (Tannis Toohey); (receiving award) The Canadian Press (Jonathan Hayward). 114–116 Photos and text courtesy of Stream of Dreams Murals Society.

Art

3-5 Illustrations reprinted by permission of Cricket Magazine Group, CarusPublishing Company from MUSE magazine February 2007, Vol. 11, No. 2, copyright © 2007 by Helen Dardik. 63–67 Illustrations by Ho Che Anderson. 107 Illustration of Jim Carrey. Charles Weiss Illustration.